Social Science for What?

Social Science for What?

Philanthropy and the Social Question in a World Turned Rightside Up

Alice O'Connor

A Russell Sage Foundation Centennial Volume

Russell Sage Foundation
New York

The Russell Sage Foundation

The Russell Sage Foundation, one of the oldest of America's general purpose foundations, was established in 1907 by Mrs. Margaret Olivia Sage for "the improvement of social and living conditions in the United States." The Foundation seeks to fulfill this mandate by fostering the development and dissemination of knowledge about the country's political, social, and economic problems. While the Foundation endeavors to assure the accuracy and objectivity of each book it publishes, the conclusions and interpretations in Russell Sage Foundation publications are those of the authors and not of the Foundation, its Trustees, or its staff. Publication by Russell Sage, therefore, does not imply Foundation endorsement.

Library of Congress Cataloging-in-Publication Data

O'Connor, Alice, 1958-
  Social science for what? : philanthropy and the social question in a world turned rightside up / Alice O'Connor

    p. cm. — (A Russell Sage Foundation centennial volume)
  Includes bibliographical references and index.
  ISBN 978-0-87154-649-4

  1. Social problems—Research—United States—History. 2. Endowments—United States. 3. Social sciences—United States. 4. United States—Social policy. 5. Liberalism—United States. 6. Conservatism—United States. 7. Russell Sage Foundation. I. Russell Sage Foundation. II. Title.

  HN57.O284 2007
  361.973072 — dc22   2006039036

The paper used in this publication meets the minimum requirements of American National Standard for Information Sciences—Permanence of Paper for Printed Library Materials. ANSI Z39.48-1992.

Text design by Suzanne Nichols.

RUSSELL SAGE FOUNDATION
112 East 64th Street, New York, New York 10021
10 9 8 7 6 5 4 3 2 1

September 24 2007

CONTENTS

About the Author

ALICE O'CONNOR is associate professor of history at the University of California, Santa Barbara.

THE RUSSELL SAGE
CENTENNIAL VOLUMES

FOREWORD

On April 19, 2007, the Russell Sage Foundation will celebrate its centennial, 100 years to the day since Margaret Olivia Sage dedicated the foundation, in her husband's name, "to the improvement of social and living conditions in the United States of America." From the outset, social research played a key role in the foundation's mission—both by providing vivid descriptions of the social problems that called out for reform in a newly industrialized, urbanized America and by assessing the effectiveness of the foundation's early programs designed to improve the lot of the disadvantaged. As the foundation's enterprise matured after World War II, the Russell Sage trustees realized that to better serve the emerging mass society social science would require significant development—in its analytic tools, its sources of data, and its theoretical capacities. Accordingly, the trustees decided that a foundation the size of RSF could contribute to the general social welfare most effectively by investing directly in the development and application of social science. This has been the foundation's unique objective ever since.

Over the past sixty years, the foundation has sought to shape and strengthen the social sciences in a wide variety of ways. It has invested in new disciplines, among them the sociology of medicine and law, and a new brand of economics based less on presumed rationality and more on evidence about how economic decisions are actually made. It has pushed to create new sources of social data, such as the General Social Survey, and to improve the analysis of existing data sources, principally by means of its long-standing analysis of social trends revealed by the U.S. Census. Russell Sage has also worked to support and disseminate promising new methodologies, such as statistical techniques for synthesizing multiple research studies of a given social policy or program to achieve more reliable generalizations about what works.

The foundation's recent activities have sustained its traditional aims of bringing social science more effectively to bear on describing social problems and analyzing the causes and consequences of social change. RSF has developed research programs on the social consequences of changing gender roles in the wake of the civil rights movement, on the vexing persistence of poverty and the rise of economic inequality in the United States over the past three decades, on the declining fortunes of minority workers in the innercity economies of the 1980s and early 1990s, and on the tectonic shifts in the U.S. labor market since the early 1980s that have put workers with limited education and bargaining power at such a distinct and growing disadvantage. Russell Sage has also devoted substantial attention to understanding the social consequences of recent demographic change. The foundation's fifteen-year program of research on the continuing wave of immigration to the United States provides a rich source of information about the impact the new immigrants are having on the country and the problems that immigrants and their children face as they try to make their way in American society. A related research program has addressed the changes in American life brought on by the increased diversity of the U.S. population—from the growing complexity of relations between racial and ethnic groups to the problems that American institutions encounter as they attempt to accommodate a more diverse citizenry.

The Russell Sage Foundation's hundredth birthday offers a unique moment to pause and take stock of this work, even as the enterprise continues. The three volumes commissioned for the centennial illustrate and reflect upon the use of social science to deepen our understanding of American life. They do not recapitulate the work of the foundation. They seek instead to push the work ahead. Over its long history, Russell Sage has struggled repeatedly to understand the social costs of the rough and tumble American labor market, the systemic roots of persistently high levels of inequality in the United States, and the political difficulties of establishing an effective role for social research in the formation of social policy.

The three centennial volumes take up these themes with innovative and provocative arguments that demonstrate again the power of social research to move debate beyond conventional wisdom, to give society fresh ways to see itself, and to recommend new strategies for improving national life. No doubt these arguments will provide rich grounds for debate. But since social science is, after all, a continuing contest founded on a shared commitment to honest evidence and reasoned argument, that is just as it should be.

Eric Wanner
President
Russell Sage Foundation

ACKNOWLEDGMENTS

For their invaluable comments and willingness to listen as I worked out the ideas in this book, I owe a great deal of thanks to Nelson Lichtenstein, Mary Furner, and Ira Katznelson. The manuscript also benefited from readings by outside reviewers, and from the research assistance of Clara Morain and Steven Attewell. I am also grateful to Suzanne Nichols of the Russell Sage Foundation, who ushered the book through the production process with a rare combination of empathy and firmness, and with the utmost professionalism. I would also like to acknowledge the Russell Sage Foundation, and Eric Wanner in particular, for making the Russell Sage Foundation centennial an occasion for broad-gauged inquiry, discussion, and reflection on the issues that have concerned the foundation throughout its history. I can only hope that this book contributes to that discussion, and somehow encourages it to continue.

INTRODUCTION

During the weeks following its founding in early spring of 1907, the Russell Sage Foundation did something that established it as a kind of unofficial keeper of the larger philanthropic idea. The foundation trustees invited critical comment from various academics and social policy intellectuals, not so much on the particulars of its yet-to-exist program as on the underlying concept of creating knowledge for "social betterment." In the ensuing decades, the foundation would make philanthropy the topic of full-fledged research programs. But it is to that original question, and in that original spirit, that my historical inquiry is cast. Its aim is to look to the past to understand the nature of the most important challenge facing that original philanthropic idea today.

At the heart of that idea was the core and enduring conviction that rational, scientific understanding of society and its problems is both a sign and an instrument of purposeful social advance.[1] The role of scientific research, as envisioned at the Russell Sage Foundation, would be to transcend personal bias, ideology, and partisan political interest to shape and inform reasoned public debate. In promoting the advancement of knowledge, private philanthropy in turn would serve not its own but an objective, discernible public interest. Equally important at the outset, the pursuit of knowledge would itself be anchored in the hope of resolving the prevailing "social question" of the day.

The concept of the social question in 1907 was very much tied to the exploited condition of labor. In fact, it was fluid enough to be able to encompass a series of questions and problems—the urban problem, the poverty problem, Henry Demarest Lloyd's problem of "Wealth Against Commonwealth," W.E.B. Du Bois's great problem of the "color line"—that all pointed to a fundamental disparity between social and economic conditions and political democracy. As such, the social question was a powerful metaphor for a wide array

1

of social problems, and, at the Russell Sage Foundation, a way of organizing its philanthropic work.

Thus, at its founding—an era of vast economic and social inequalities and a deepening ideological and political divide—the Russell Sage Foundation would look to social research as an essential instrument in the work of ameliorative social reform. The content of that work would be heavily empirical, but its framing of the issues would be ideological as well as practical. In this instance, it would carve out the boundaries of a diversified, often internally conflicted "new liberalism" within the vast space between laissez-faire and socialist extremes.[2] As a first order of business, it would take hold of and reframe the social question to emphasize its roots in objective social and economic conditions that were themselves amenable to reform. It was this effort to, in effect, socialize the social question that most consistently linked the new philanthropy to the progressive as well as the longer new liberal reform tradition, and that would eventually draw it into the orbit of the New Deal.

Later, taking a new approach to the social question, the Russell Sage Foundation would remake itself. It would do so within an emerging tradition of philanthropic knowledge-building that, in the context of cold war and widening postwar affluence, became increasingly detached from the immediacy of reform politics and the social question, even as its ambitions for social science grew. Although couched once again in the neutralizing language of advancing knowledge and promoting the public interest, these ambitions were keyed to the needs of post–World War II liberalism, now struggling to construct a political and ideological program that would reconcile its incomplete commitments to racial justice and economic security with the global crusade against communism.[3] Philanthropy would contribute to this project of reconciliation with a massive expansion of theoretical and applied research. The theoretical was to focus on behavioral and cultural theories of democracy, social stratification, and economic modernization; the applied on reducing social problems to containable root causes that could in turn be resolved through existing institutions of civil society, the private market, and—most of all—enlightened government policy.

Of course, in claiming theirs to be an apolitical, nonideological purpose, foundations were exercising a degree of political and ideological control, not in the least by treating key tenets of the so-called liberal consensus as beyond ideological contention, but especially by circumscribing the boundaries of public debate. For this, they would come under persistent criticism, and calls for federal regulation, from both the McCarthyite right and the social democratic left. Meanwhile, philanthropic influence would be more visibly reflected in the vast institutionalization of ideologically neutral expertise in policy think tanks and government agencies, and in the politics of knowledge that established their empirical, problem-solving approach as the dominant mode of policy and policy-relevant social scientific research. Though dwarfed by the expansion of federal contracts and research funding, foundations continued to serve as a kind of linchpin in the postwar liberal research and policy establishment.

Now, in an era once again marked by growing inequality and a deep political and ideological divide, this philanthropic tradition finds itself in a state of uncertainty, if not crisis, as it confronts the challenges of a world "turned rightside up."[4] One major challenge is the prospect of its own political and cultural irrelevance. This prospect is occasioned equally by the rise of the ideological right—with its denigration of big government, its hostility to the idea of an independent public purpose, its increasingly blatant subordination of science to a combination of corporate interest and Christian fundamentalist faith, and its revival of such once-presumed settled battles in the scientific culture wars as the teaching of Darwinian evolution—and by the seemingly permanent demise of liberalism as a viable political ideology. A second challenge is the relentless rise of economic, social, and political inequality since the 1980s, and its virtual absence, despite reams of social research documenting the dimensions and consequences of growing inequality, as an issue in public debate. Third, and what brings the others most directly into focus, is the growing power and influence of an entirely alternative, explicitly conservative, philanthropic tradition, and the self-consciously "counterrevolutionary" research and policy estab-

3

lishment it has helped to create. These challenges, and what they mean for the tradition of philanthropy and social research the Russell Sage Foundation represents, are the subject of this book.

What This Book Is About

Social Science for What? is a historical inquiry into the early roots of the philanthropic project of creating social science in the public interest and the more recent transformations that now confront it with a challenge to its founding premises. As suggested by its partly but deliberately borrowed title, the book is a critical inquiry into a much-needed debate about whether and how this philanthropic project is capable of meeting its self-appointed responsibilities at a critical moment for social knowledge and for liberal democracy. As befitting the occasion of the Russell Sage Foundation's centenary, it is also meant as an invitation to revisit longstanding debates over questions of value and neutrality in socially purposeful social scientific research.

The source of the title is, of course, Robert Lynd's classic *Knowledge for What?* a book rightly renowned as a classic of American social thought and social science, and a call for socially engaged research.[5] Writing in the 1930s amid the global crises of war, totalitarianism, and economic collapse, Lynd issued an impassioned plea for a more fully relevant social knowledge, a knowledge willing to cut through the reigning mythology and prejudices of American culture—among which Lynd included the myths of equal opportunity, free market individualism, and the self-regulating market—to clear the way for enlightened social change. He also issued a warning about the dangers of a social science trapped within the confines of narrow empiricism and overly abstracted theory, and sheltered behind the veil of neutral scholarly detachment. Such a science, he argued, was both all too willing to accept prevailing definitions of social problems and incapable of questioning prevailing social norms. Such a science was failing to meet its broader responsibilities—at a moment when what society needed more than anything was a fearless and penetrating inquiry into the viability of its most cherished, but outdated, values and institutions.

By invoking Lynd in our own, albeit far different, historical moment, I wish to emphasize the urgency of the issues that philanthropy and social research now face. I also wish to underscore the degree to which those issues are rooted in deep-seated historical conflicts, over the value and indeed the scientific validity of strict neutrality in social scientific research, and over the struggle to envision and create a more genuinely democratic knowledge. I aim to underscore the degree to which the current crisis is cultural as well as political and ideological, involving, as it does, ongoing conflict over the cultural orientation of American society—and whether it needs or is even subject to change.

I highlight these themes in the first two chapters of the book, where I locate the historical origins of the philanthropic project in a far different, more explicitly purposive and reformist vision of social science than the one we have grown familiar with today. That vision was most fully embodied in the early Russell Sage Foundation and in the pathbreaking research it initiated with the famous Pittsburgh Survey and in a substantial body of original research through the Great Depression. I then turn to consider and revisit the highly contested debates that accompanied the eventual eclipse of that original Progressive-era vision, and that came to a height with the publication of Lynd's *Knowledge for What?* (1939) and Gunnar Myrdal's *An American Dilemma* (1944). Once again, the course of the early reform vision was captured by the Russell Sage Foundation, which in 1947 announced a fundamental shift in emphasis from social reform to social science.

I am equally concerned, however, with what is historically distinctive about the current challenges, and with whether philanthropy and social research as currently constituted are capable of an effective response. I thus shift gears in the second part of the book to offer an interpretive narrative of the historical rise of the conservative research and policy establishment starting in the immediate post–World War II years, emphasizing its roots in an alternative philanthropic tradition as well as an alternative, distinctively conservative tradition of social knowledge and political philosophy.

As I show in chapters 3 through 5, four aspects distinguish this as an alternative philanthropic tradition. First is its belief that philanthropy should be both ideological and forthright about its ideological commitments—to economic and cultural conservativism, and to the not always compatible values of limited government, free-market capitalism, individualism, and traditional (Victorian) virtue. Second, and related, is its advocacy of a reform program based on the similarly conflicted principles of extreme economic deregulation and heightened moral regulation—in particular for poor and otherwise socially marginalized groups. Third, and indeed what binds the internally conflicting strands of this reform agenda, is right-wing philanthropy's insistence on desocializing as well as moralizing the social question—in the sense of holding individuals personally responsible for their disadvantages—and on the personally redemptive power of free markets in the necessarily moral response. Fourth is its engagement in what conservatives often refer to as the war of ideas, but is more accurately described as a sustained attack on the so-labeled liberal, nominally nonideological research and policy establishment and its nominally nonideological philanthropic sponsors.

My narrative traces how these overlapping commitments have come together over the past three decades in the form of an organized movement to build a foundation-funded conservative "counterintelligentsia" based on a strategy memorably described by former Treasury Secretary William Simon as to provide "grants, grants and more grants in exchange for books, books and more books."[6] Along with other central themes, it highlights the importance of formerly left-liberal neoconservative intellectuals in this philanthropic countermovement, and of their attention to the cultural as well as the political and ideological fronts. Their efforts are very much reflected in the major intellectual achievements outlined in a recent insider's retrospective of three decades of conservative philanthropic activism. Among them are supply-side economics, the law and economics movement, Charles Murray's blueprint for the "end of welfare," and the galvanizing effect of such missives in the academic culture wars as Allan Bloom's *The Closing of the American Mind* and Dinesh D'Souza's *Illiberal Education.*[7] Such inroads are but a part of the sweeping reconfiguration of the policy research and advocacy landscape that has occurred over the past three decades, with the emergence of a wide network of richly endowed conservative "advocacy tanks." [8]

If all of these highlight the blatantly oppositional nature of the right-wing philanthropic movement, I also focus on its successful introduction of a characteristically conservative kind of knowledge into social policy and public debates. What distinguishes this as conservative knowledge is not simply that it is driven by ideological, partisan concerns, or that it is associated with conservative institutes and think tanks. Rather, it is that the knowledge stems from a fundamentally different philosophy of knowledge, only recently associated with the University of Chicago philosopher Leo Strauss, and what conservatives consider to be unimpeachable truths. On the one hand is the idea that civilized society works according to certain universal standards of human behavior and morality that transcend both place and time. On the other is that social "pathologies" stem from bad behavior, from culturally "relativist" attitudes, and especially from permissive liberal policies that have encouraged broad cultural decay. This is not the kind of knowledge that can be derived from empirical inquiry. Although frequently couched in the conventions of empirical social science, it is both suspicious and subversive of the empirical, philosophically pragmatic, morally (in conservatives' eyes) relativist tradition of liberal policy research.[9] It is instead drawn from ideas that conservatives treat as objective, established fact: about the superiority of free market capitalism, the two-parent patriarchal family, and ancient and Victorian-era virtues (a term they prefer over *values* because it conveys less contingency and more of an air of objective reality).[10]

Using one illustration of the distinctive nature and growing power of conservative social knowledge, I focus in chapter 4 on the role of such knowledge in the 1970s and in the precursor to the welfare reform debate. For one thing, Charles Murray and other analysts associated with conservative think tanks have proved entirely willing to use statistical manipulation and factual distortion to suit their ideological purposes, even while seeming to participate in the numbers-crunching and data-mining that is common currency in the trade. But the more basic point is that, despite claims to the contrary, they do not accept the seemingly neutral idea that knowledge based on empirical research should inform policy decisions. Instead, they seek to engage the issues on the altogether different plane of ideas and principles that lie beyond the reach of evidentiary exposition.[11] In the end, the lack of statistical evidence that welfare payments promote single motherhood does not matter. What does matter is that welfare tolerates single motherhood by softening the economic hardship that single motherhood otherwise would—and in a moral society should—impose. Or, as Murray puts it in one of many Malthusian descriptions of the evil of welfare, it "enables women to bear children without the natural social restraints."[12] Empirical social science, by seeking to resolve a moral issue based on statistical evidence, actually obscures a higher truth: that society should not be subsidizing the evil of unwed motherhood. As the example of welfare shows, then, the standard of conservative knowledge is not empirical rigor or soundness, but adherence to higher truth. Social policy is not the only thing that needs to be remoralized. Social knowledge does as well.

A final, key point I make in discussing the distinctive nature of conservative social and policy knowledge centers on the purposes it is meant to serve: not so much those of investigation and pragmatic problem-solving as those of movement building. This is reflected in the emphasis on values and on core, unifying ideas, and in the highly effective idea-marketing strategies for which the right has been renowned. It is reflected as well in the use of ideas—literally—as weapons in the policy and culture wars. But it is perhaps most fully manifest in the degree to which conservative knowledge focuses on providing the movement with a usable past, an account of the origins of a wide range of contemporary social policy problems based on a simplistically coherent, highly distorted, endlessly repeated narrative that holds not only Great Society but also the whole of twentieth-century liberalism responsible for an era of economic decline and cultural dissolution dating from the 1960s, all in anticipation of the immanent triumph of ascendant conservatism.

I conclude part II with a discussion of the substantial progress that conservative philanthropy has made in the crusade to establish what we might call a more faith-based, movement-oriented social knowledge. Such progress is abundantly clear in the veritable beachhead of tightly networked foundations, think tanks, and values-oriented research institutes established around the country in recent years.[13] It is also clear in the extent to which the language and categories of conservative social knowledge have become institutionalized in the public sector as well as in public debate, as evidenced by the proliferation of federally sponsored marriage and family values initiatives, along with the several offices of faith-based and community initiatives in the White House and in federal, state, and intergovernmental bureaucracies. These and other right-wing triumphs speak as much to the effectiveness of the broader conservative coalition as they do to the effectiveness of its philanthropic branch.

My account, however, also attributes the growing power and influence of conservative philanthropy to the corresponding incapacitation of its more centrist as well as its progressive-liberal counterparts. Perhaps most telling in this regard are the lengths to which historically liberal and nominally nonideological foundations and think tanks have gone to accommodate, and in the process to empower, conservative social knowledge in the postwelfare debate, as the inclusion of Charles Murray in a recent Brookings volume and a number of other efforts to ensure ideological balance in research and policy analysis suggest.[14] These balancing acts are justified as efforts to be fair-minded in laying out and airing the key issues for debate. In reality, and especially in the case of welfare, they have done more to validate the conservative reform agenda and skew how the issues are formulated to the right. In the first place, they have unquestioningly adopted conservative categories of analysis—dependency, self-sufficiency, illegitimacy—as if these categories have no moral or ideological content. Second, even when they acknowledge their differences on specific issues, the admittedly liberal contributors to these projects fail to engage conservative values and ideological premises in any critical way. Instead, they assess the so-labeled higher truths posited by conservative positions exclusively on empirical grounds. Third, in presenting theirs as a comprehensive airing of the issues, they have effectively marginalized, if not silenced, significant critical voices, along with the issues—entitlement, rights, caregiving work, economic justice—that have been raised outside a highly circumscribed set of policy options.

I conclude by returning to themes and debates discussed in the first part of the book, to outline a more socially purposive approach to research that respects the principle of open-minded, unbiased inquiry, that acknowledges the values behind its research commitments and priorities, and that uses those values to both reframe old questions and ask new ones. Here I focus on drawing insights (which is not to say direct lessons or strategies to be imitated) not, as others have, from the conservative counterrevolution, but (and more important) from the earlier, progressive approach to philanthropy and research. Once again echoing Robert Lynd, I end by discussing the role of philanthropy in knowledge that reframes the social question and looks beyond elite circles to the broader society. Although I offer answers, my aim in raising these questions is to engage in a necessarily collective, more inclusive conversation about what a more democratic and socially relevant approach to knowledge looks like, and how we begin to get there from here.

PART I

RECONNECTING TO THE PROGRESSIVE PAST

৶ CHAPTER 1 ৶

ENGAGING THE SOCIAL QUESTION AT THE EARLY RUSSELL SAGE FOUNDATION

The Pittsburgh Survey has been a rapid, close range investigation of living conditions in the Pennsylvania steel district. . . . It has been made practicable by co-operation from two quarters—from a remarkable group of leaders and organizations in social and sanitary movements in different parts of the United States, who entered upon the field work as a piece of national good citizenship; and from men, women and organizations in Pittsburgh who were large-minded enough to regard their local situation as not private and peculiar, but a part of the American problem of city building.
   —Paul U. Kellogg, "The Pittsburgh Survey"

You have heard of Shakespeare's London, of the port of Lisbon in the days of the Spanish Main, of the mixtures of caste and race and faith on the trade routes of the East. They are of the ilk of Pittsburgh. How to get orderly plans of social betterment out of the study of such a community is at first sight a staggering question. But the clue to its answer is that same fact that stood out when we looked at Pittsburgh as a city of tonnage and incandescence. These people are here to work. This fact once grasped in its bearings and we get a foot hold for estimating Pittsburgh. The wage earners become a fairly well-defined belt in the population. What the issues of life and labor mean to

> them will help us in understanding the trend of conditions in industrial communities generally.
> —Paul U. Kellogg, "The Pittsburgh Survey"[1]

I open with these passages from the Pittsburgh Survey because they come from a social science that mattered in its capacity to capture and make a difference in the central issues of its time. Here we see encapsulated what gave the study its resonance within the broader culture: ethnographic observation that spoke eloquently to the work and family lives of Pittsburgh's wage earners; photographs that, in visually capturing the essence of the analysis, both animated and extended the boundaries of what constituted social scientific data; and a clear sense of the public purpose of social science and its responsibility to illuminate the social question as asked and experienced by the citizens of a modern industrial democracy. All this falls within the parameters of an empirical social investigation, framed by survey director Paul U. Kellogg in the expansive language of social citizenship and visualized in the imagery of a shared civic understanding of the social question that has yet to be resolved (see figure 1.1).

The Pittsburgh Survey, of course, was the first, and best known, major research project the Russell Sage Foundation funded. It was a massive investigation of "life and labor" in the urban, immigrant, and—above all—industrial Pittsburgh of 1907 and 1908. It relied on scores of researchers, community volunteers, and the social photography of Lewis Hine to bring out the essential humanity and the dignity of labor as it revealed the human cost of economic inequality, poverty, and social neglect. Mostly, in the words of the survey report, it relied on "unbiased" scientific investigation of the "social facts" for a purpose that certainly speaks to us today: to engage a broad, and broadly public conversation about the future of liberal democracy in an age of unbridled corporate capitalism.

Later I will return to the question of how, and how well, the Pittsburgh Survey succeeded in these aims. For the moment, I note that it was widely regarded as the most important sociological project of

Figure 1.1   Scheme of the Pittsburgh Survey

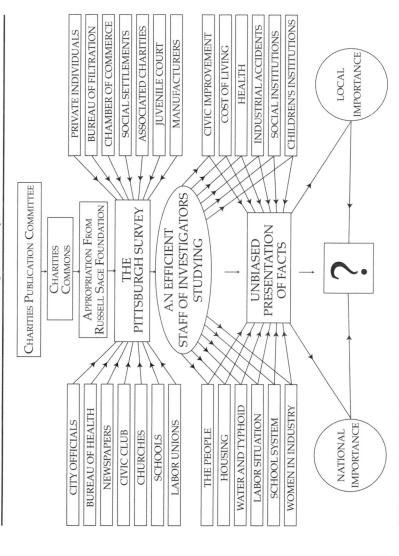

Source: Pittsburgh Civic Exhibit, Carnegie Institute, November–December, 1908. Reproduced from Kellogg (1909, 519).

the day. It was innovative, thoroughly documented, astonishingly comprehensive, and helped jump start what would be enduring reform discussions about measures such as workers' compensation and shortening the twelve-hour day, seven-day work week still widely practiced in American industry at the time. That judgment has subsequently been confirmed by historians, who turn to the Survey both as a rich source of data for working class life at turn of the century and for insight into the attitudes and beliefs shaping Progressive-era research and reform. Moreover, by putting things on the table that hadn't been there before, its scope and methods helped to lay essential groundwork for future research and policy investigation on an extraordinarily broad range of issues. These include workplace conditions, ethnic stratification of the labor force, the changing meaning of "women's work" at home and in the industrial workforce, the causes and consequences of environmental degradation, and the use of law in social policy—and household strategies to fill the gap between income and need. Indeed, looking back over a century, it is hard *not* to be struck with how much the central preoccupations of the Survey—the social costs of getting a living on "$1.65 a day," the challenges of organizing a labor force that was global in origin if not location, the political and civic consequences of widening economic insecurity and concentrated wealth—resonate with current concerns about growing inequality.

And yet the legacy of the Pittsburgh Survey and its ongoing relevance go largely unrecognized in social science today. To be sure, it is occasionally commemorated—or dismissed—as an example of reformist progressive investigation at its height. It has also been taken to task—and not without reason—for its middle-class prejudices, its tone of condescension, and its hints of disapproval in even sympathetic depictions of the predominantly Slavic immigrant working class. But, for the most part, whether in praise or criticism, the Pittsburgh Survey and the tradition of reform investigation it stands for have been relegated in the social scientific imagination to a safe and distant past. My aim here, then, is not to offer a full-blown historical assessment. That is a larger and necessarily ongoing project, to which others have contributed and will no doubt return as cities like

Pittsburgh continue to grapple with the consequences of globalization and industrial restructuring.[2] My aim instead is to reconnect to that part of its past that has to do with how the Russell Sage Foundation originally conceptualized its sense of public purpose and to suggest its enduring relevance to the contemporary project of creating "social science that matters" in the broader public sphere. At stake is not simply the Pittsburgh Survey or the social survey as a form of social inquiry, though that offers a great deal worth recovering. The animating vision of a purposive, engaged social science the survey represents is at stake as well—a vision the Russell Sage Foundation cultivated and became a leading institutional home for on its founding in 1907 and for much of its first century. That is worth revisiting as the foundation enters its second.

In that vision, played out in hundreds of social surveys, community and case studies, and investigatory inquiries funded by a number of private and public agencies through the 1930s, social research could and should be rigorously objective and empirical as well as socially purposive. Research would draw on social facts rather than existing doctrines to uncover the root causes of social problems and inequities. It would be an expert-led and scientifically directed endeavor, but not an exclusively academic or otherwise professionalized one. At its most expansive and idealized, social scientific inquiry would involve a large, a varied, and an amateur as well as an expert public in gathering, learning from, debating, publicizing, and ultimately acting on the implications of the social facts. Social science, though rigorous and unbiased by class or narrowly partisan interests, would not be detached or disengaged from the political struggles, debates, and looming social questions of its time. Its aim would not simply be better knowledge about social conditions or about programs for social betterment, but to produce knowledge that would open up new ways of thinking about society, social problems, and what could be achieved by democratic governance as well as new ideas for more targeted political and social reforms. The role of such research would be to broaden rather than to confine itself to the existing realm of political possibility—to stimulate and expand the democratic policy imagination. Ultimately, as envisioned by a significant cadre of progressive intellectuals, more inclusive models of scientific inquiry and education—social surveys, worker education institutes, and Jane Addams's Working People's Social Science Club—would play a central role in creating a more inclusive set of policy conversations, a more democratic polity and culture, in the parlance of more contemporary democratic theory, a democratic public sphere.[3]

There is some irony and poignancy, of course, in the fact that the distancing from this reformist vision of social science was most fully symbolized in the sudden (at least to grantees) but deliberate shift in the Russell Sage Foundation's program emphasis—from social amelioration and reform inquiry to academic social science—just after World War II. In reality, the complex of factors undermining that earlier vision, including more decisive shifts in philanthropic preference toward academic, professionalized, and putatively neutral or apolitical social science, had begun at least two decades earlier. Those shifts have in turn been naturalized and perpetuated in a particular, much-criticized but still widely influential narrative of social scientific development that splits the past into two disconnected phases, if indeed it even recognizes the roots of social science in a broader reform tradition. The first phase is seen as well-meaning but comparatively soft and amateur, more feminized, oriented toward social work and charity. The second is presumably more rigorously scientific, academic, masculinized, and professional. In that narrative, social science is seen as having become progressively more scientific, objective, and ideologically neutral as a byproduct of methodological and theoretical advance—and because of having long since separated itself from the naïve reformism of socially ameliorative research. Indeed, viewed from the narrative of a progressively more scientific and professionalized social science, the intellectuals and reformers who populated the early RSF research community were not only unscientific. They were politically irrelevant as well. Their efforts were at best a kind of amateurish precursor to what would emerge as a more recognizable social science in the expanding research universities of the late 1910s and 1920s, and in an empirical science of economy, society, and governance that could guide social policy and practice toward predictable ends. Moreover, their vision of cultivating such an enlightened democratic public is seen as politically naïve. Most important, infused and motivated as they were by an essentially moral, if not overtly political, commitment to reform, the largely extra-academic investigations and the research and reform networks that the early RSF sponsored are seen to have lacked the legitimacy and scientific authority of their presumably more neutral and academic counterparts. Thus would the RSF shift to a more neutral social science be accompanied by a powerfully symbolic physical relocation, out of the New York City (and national) social work and reform corridor it had anchored with its monumental Florentine building and into a more socially anonymous, behind-the-scenes habitat.

I begin, then, with an alternative account of social investigation at the early Russell Sage Foundation that challenges this narrative of a progressively more scientific and neutral social science in several ways. First, I argue that contemporary social science has a great deal to learn from the Pittsburgh Survey and other early investigations: from their methods and their multifaceted and often imaginative approach, from their efforts to engage with both a broader public and the people they were learning about, and from the kinds of questions they were willing and able to ask. On one level, this means reconnecting to a neglected tradition of social inquiry. Indeed, it is striking how much of the methodological insight and innovation of early social science—having been forgotten, or overlooked, or not taken seriously as science—has subsequently been discovered or reinvented by later generations of academically trained researchers. The periodic invocation of the need to integrate qualitative and quantitative methods, fieldwork and statistical analysis, is but one example. More to the larger point of my argument, however, is what contemporary social science has to gain by reconnecting to the tradition of engaging the social question in a way that opens a conversation about how society can act collectively to realize its aspirations as a liberal democracy. To do that requires coming to terms with, and acknowledging, its understanding of what those aspirations are and being willing to subject that understanding to scrutiny as part of public discourse.

Second, my account is based on an understanding of social science as fully a part of the broader society and culture it purports to make sense of—not as a body of knowledge that can be understood independent of its historical context, or of the politics, social experience, prevailing (even if hidden or unconscious) cultural prejudices and norms, and available funding that play a role in determining the questions social scientists are and are not asking at any given time. This is not to say that social science cannot or should not reasonably aspire to standards of scientific objectivity such as empirical accuracy, plausibility, and, when appropriate, verifiability by independent tests and critical reviews of its findings. These are all standards to which the Pittsburgh surveyors aspired and to a large degree achieved. It can and should, however, recognize that pure objectivity is impossible. Social science involves human judgments and value decisions at every stage, from the questions asked to the methods used to answer those questions, to underlying assumptions about the way the world does, and should, work.

Third, and along these same lines, social science at the early Russell Sage Foundation reminds us that neutrality is not some fixed and timeless standard but a historically contingent concept. That is, it is shaped over time by changing—and continually contested—ideas about what constitutes scientific objectivity and who is capable of being objective, by the changing scope and aspirations of social science as a profession and as a field of inquiry, and by institutional designations of what can be considered neutral that have themselves been defined within the boundaries of a shifting political and social status quo. Research at the early RSF emerged at a time and within an institutional space when the practices and norms of social scientific inquiry were being learned as much in the college settlements, social movements, tenement house and factory inspections, and public bureau inquiries as in the research university. It thus made its most significant contributions to social scientific knowledge because of, not in spite of, its origins in reform. Not by coincidence, the early RSF also made substantial social scientific contributions as one of the leading career and training grounds for a generation of pioneering women researchers, and as a venue for generating knowledge about women and work. Standards of neutrality, by contrast, emerged within the context of the quest for professionalization and scientific legitimacy within the social sciences, developments that contributed to narrowed opportunities for women in research.[4] Especially consequential, standards of neutrality became most fully institutionalized in social science and philanthropy under structural and historical circumstances that simply no longer apply. To the degree that neutrality in social research can be said to have had its moment, it coincided with the brief period of what appeared to be widely shared prosperity and ideological consensus following World War II. The moment was one in which the country's most prominent social scientists assumed that the broad outlines of the social question had for all intents and purposes been permanently settled within the framework of a New Deal social contract and a Keynesian political economy. That assumption—as socially and economically disenfranchised African Americans, women, poor people and others knew at the time, and has become powerfully evident with the rise of the new right—was wrong.

Fourth, my discussion picks up on an insight drawn from a great deal of scholarship on the historical development of social science and its changing role in influencing public debates. That scholarship tells us that social science has been shaped and continually reshaped in periods of political and ideological crisis and change. At the early RSF this meant the immediate crises of late Gilded Age poverty and wealth, of two major wartime mobilizations, and of the Great Depression and the near collapse of capitalism. For African American scholars, it was the enduring crisis of race and democracy that gave title to the NAACP journal edited by W.E.B. Du Bois. Within the field more broadly, it was the series of crises precipitated by mass industrialization, capitalist reorganization, and racial conflict beginning in the mid-nineteenth century, straight through to the current challenges before liberal democracies in an era of global economic restructuring, rising inequality, and fears over terrorist threats. In these and in similarly reorienting moments of change and crisis, social scientific inquiry played a normative and ideological as well as an empirical and theory-generating role: by offering, or attempting to offer, new ways of thinking about the relationships between the state, markets, and civil society, and about social problems and what could be done about them; and by highlighting the disparities between social ideals and realities.

Moreover, as we also know from a great deal of historical scholarship, social science for most of its history has been oriented to the needs of what at the time were thought of and talked about as a series of new liberalisms preoccupied by questions of state and social citizenship—preoccupations more recently displaced by a highly individualistic, anti-statist, and market-oriented neoliberalism.[5]

Finally, my account uses early Russell Sage Foundation research to argue that it is possible to be socially purposive and clear about acknowledging the value commitments that motivate research while respecting the norms of rigorous empirical inquiry—to recognize, as the historian Thomas Haskell puts it, that objectivity and neutrality are not the same.[6] Social scientific (in which I would include historical) inquiry thrives on the constant give and take between interpretive theories, hypotheses, ideas, and evidence, and in the necessarily ongoing critical discourse that subjects findings, interpretations, and conclusions to evidence-based argumentation and scrutiny. Nor should we diminish the importance and broader cultural value of such factually informed debate, especially as we now witness the consequences of the rise of an overtly faith- and ideology-based style of politics and policy decision making.[7] But to conclude that social scientists or the institutions that fund them lose legitimacy in acknowledging their ideological assumptions and roots in political philosophy is to miss a larger, crucial point. The movement that brought us the so-called faith-based style of politics rests on a challenge not only to the empirical research tradition but also to its essentially normative foundational ideas—including the belief, as I will discuss, in a positive public purpose beyond the narrow limits of preserving free market principles and policing the public order. It is also to cut contemporary social science off from what made that earlier generation of RSF-affiliated social scientists effective, and with a more nuanced approach than we currently acknowledge—the normative purposes that shaped, and ultimately enhanced and gave social meaning to their empirical research, among other ways, by generating otherwise unasked questions and stimulating new ways of thinking about the problems of and prospects for a more just society.

Social Science, Ideology, and Reform

Although it is often framed in terms of a stark and stylized opposition—as handed to us from Max Weber, "value-free" versus "normative" research—the concept of neutrality has been continually debated and redefined as a standard in social science, and as a strategy for establishing relevance and legitimacy. More important for purposes of my discussion, this debate took place within a framework of shared assumptions and value commitments that joined the diverse array of academics, policy intellectuals, labor and social welfare activists, religious leaders, and philanthropists who were behind late nineteenth- and early-twentieth-century efforts to make social scientific knowledge a guidepost in public life. Rooted in the conviction that the changes society was experiencing had rendered old ways of thinking and knowing obsolete, the shared assumptions underlying early social science can be considered ideological in four key respects—each of which, as we shall see, have figured centrally in the challenge from the ideological right. First of these is embracing what at the time was a self-consciously modernist way of understanding and viewing the world—one that implicitly and controversially rejected the authority of revealed truth and received doctrine in favor of a more contingent, empirical approach. Second is providing the basis for a distinctively scientific approach to understanding social change—an approach that would again prove controversial in its insistence that the huge social and economic changes, disparities, and conflicts manifest in modern industrial capitalism were not part of some mysterious, naturally unfolding process but instead subject to scientific management if not more fundamental reform. Third is in reimagining what John Dewey called "the public and its problems" as interdependent, collective, and social rather than individual and private, and as embedded in a similarly collective and interdependent "public interest" that transcended the divisions of class, politically partisan, or otherwise particularistic interests. Fourth is in offering, or hoping to offer, a framework in which to evaluate and reimagine existing political and economic arrangements—specifically those justified by laissez-faire doctrine—within a larger sense of public purpose. It is in this last dimension that what can loosely be described as a social scientific ideology is most nearly mapped onto familiar categories of political ideology. For in their social policy imaginings, practitioners of the new social knowledge traveled within, and helped to trace out, the boundaries of a new liberalism that recognized the need to control the forces of market and social transformation but left a wide swath for negotiating the particulars of what such control would mean.

As we can see, then, early social science was ideological in the loosest sense. Within the broad boundaries of the new liberalism, it accommodated pluralistic politics and competing visions of public purpose and the common good. Indeed, if it was doctrinaire about anything, it was about the need to avoid blind adherence to doctrine in interpreting social facts. In this, early social science showed the influence of John Dewey and philosophical pragmatism, with its commitment to finding truth—and principles for public policy—in lived experience and experimentation rather than in fixed and unchanging precepts. It also left much to be debated, if not resolved, certainly about the big social questions regarding state and society, labor and capital, and race, but also about how to define the public interest and the role of social science in that task. Neither, however, was it utterly relativistic, as conservative critics would come to charge. Again in the broadest sense, and especially in its approach to the social question, social science defined itself in the search for the principles—scientific and normative—for a modernized liberal democracy.[8]

Notably, neutrality per se was not a bedrock principle of social science, which from the start was heavily influenced by the Social Gospel and by explicitly moral concerns about the dominance of an increasingly cruel and competitive form of capitalism in American life. Moreover, as discussed further in chapter two, the notion of a value-free social science was subject to ongoing debate among social scientists very much wedded to the norms of empirical research. Indeed, the institutionalized concern with what a later writer would call neutralism became more acute only later, as foundations and research institutions sought, on the one hand, to hold themselves above or apart from the political controversies surrounding the research they funded (and the "tainted money" behind it) and on the other to "speak truth" to the reigning political establishment. The advantage, henceforth, would be with social science that could be couched in politically neutral terms, that emphasized technical proficiency, and that avoided more fundamental and potentially radical questions about the existing social order.

It is also important to recognize that, for so much in that congeries of problems that comprised the social question, systematic social research was the work of reform: not so much in affiliating itself with a particular reform program as in its capacity to lay bare the distance between social values and social reality. Nowhere was this more the case, as W.E.B. Du Bois insisted in his early career, than in the case of the so-called "Negro Problem." There the search for the "simple truth" was so heavily resisted by the power of "the manifest and far-reaching bias of writers," of the preference for acting on "faith" rather than "knowledge," and of "the widespread conviction among Americans that no persons of Negro descent should become constituent members of the social body." The weight of resistance, indeed, made it that much more important for reform-minded science to stick to the "ascertainment of the facts" so that society might "settle its problems in accordance with its highest ideals."[9] This was an approach that, after decades of conducting empirical surveys of Negro life and labor, Du Bois would abandon as inadequate. Understanding the depths of American racism would require a more psychological, historical, and a more ideologically purposeful approach, if for no other reason than to confront how deeply implicated scientific knowledge of all kinds had become in racial hatred and white supremacy.[10]

Neutrality was surely not the paramount concern when Margaret Olivia Sage established the Russell Sage Foundation in 1907 as what is widely regarded as the first large-scale, professionally staffed, general purpose foundation in the United States. Nor, technically, was social scientific research. Mrs. Sage's mandate was purposely open-ended and, as legend would have it, a comeuppance of sorts for her late husband's ferocity in making, and clinging to

25

his vast railroad and speculative fortune. Fiorello La Guardia called Russell Sage "one of the meanest skinflints who ever lived."[11] "Mrs. Sage," in the fantastically understated words of RSF's first official chronicle, on inheriting his entire fortune—estimated at $65 million—in 1906, "immediately began giving away the millions [Russell Sage] had accumulated."[12] The foundation's stated purpose was "the improvement of social and living conditions in the United States of America," and research was but one of the many possible approaches the trustees—Olivia Sage among them—were free to pursue. The foundation's physical presence only underscored the point. Research at the early Russell Sage Foundation was literally encased within a massive Italian Renaissance–style building that Olivia Sage had designed as a tribute to the sometimes competing strands of direct charity, social scientific investigation, and secularized religion that shaped the foundation's aims. Physically embedded in a series of carved panels was an unmistakable message: "service" was the centerpiece of the building's ornate arched entryway, flanked by "study and counsel." Other panels carved into the building's façade celebrated the values of work, play, health, housing, education, justice, and religion—the last reading "He that Doeth Good is of God."[13]

The building's ornamentation, though, spoke as much to the unity as to the potential tensions within the foundation's mission, to a time when the lines between research and reform were not as rigid as they would later become, and when much of the work of social science grew out of the concerns of the social gospel. Seen in this light, it is not so surprising that research became the centerpiece of the foundation's reform activities, which spanned child welfare, education, housing, "women's work," consumer credit, urban planning, and charity organization. In fact, it was in the course of such broad-gauged reform work that RSF became a kind of institutional headquarters and standard bearer for objective yet normative and politically engaged social scientific research.

Ultimately, it was no single one but the combination of research and reform commitments that led one scholarly reviewer, writing in the *American Sociological Review,* to call the Pittsburgh Survey the most "important single enterprise in the field of social investigation. . . undertaken in the [United States]." Although launched when the RSF was still embryonic, the Pittsburgh Survey remains the most comprehensive expression of its purposive social science, both in the scope of the inquiry and in its embeddedness in a larger, longer, more sustained and broadly public conversation about social policy, public philosophy, and the possibilities for reform.

The first thing to note about the Pittsburgh Survey is that it was hugely ambitious, propelled by the growing momentum within progressive reform circles and by their faith in the power of knowledge to make the looming and still inchoate social question intelligible to a diversified if not to say divided polity. This ambition comes through all the more clearly in light of the survey's apparently modest start. This was nothing more than a 1906 letter from Alice B. Montgomery, chief probation officer of Pittsburgh's Allegheny County, suggesting that the journal then known as *Charities and the Commons* take up an investigation of social conditions in Pittsburgh as a follow-up to its recent, widely regarded report on neglected neighborhoods in the nation's capital. Within months, that request had grown into a massive, year-long inquiry into the whole of working-class life in industrial Pittsburgh, thanks in no small part to the journal's connections in progressive reform circles. Although still relatively new and with a small but growing circulation of approximately 10,000, the journal was also a creation of the consolidating charity organization, settlement house, and social work networks that came together under the rubric of the Charities Publication Committee, based at New York's influential Charity Organization Society. Heading up the committee was an impressive board of advisers that included such reform luminaries as Jane Addams and social journalist and photographer Jacob Riis. More important from the standpoint of financing the survey, though, was the influence of the committee's founder, Olivia Sage's well-connected lawyer and soon-to-be RSF board vice president (and later president) Robert W. de Forest. With such social and financial capital at hand, and seed money that eventually turned into the foundation's first major ($27,000) research grant, journal editor Paul U. Kellogg recruited the likes of labor economist John R. Commons, National Consumers League founder Florence Kelley, and settlement house movement leader Robert Woods for an independent advisory board. But what truly catalyzed the investigation into a full-fledged social scientific survey was that nested within all these social reform networks was a tremendous store of intellectual capital that could be organized virtually overnight. Each of these networks, after all, was steeped in a tradition of social scientific reform investigation of its own—the settlement house in the social survey; Florence Kelley's National Consumers' League in factory inspection; charity organization societies in household budget surveys and tenement house investigations; labor organizations in wage, workplace, and standard of living surveys—and in the emerging research traditions of Wisconsin School instititutionalist economics.

The Pittsburgh Survey's roots in reform thus brought a considerable intellectual as well as activist ambition to the investigation, enough to attract scores of professional and amateur researchers, many from elsewhere in the United States, and many for up to a year. Under Kellogg's direction, their joint efforts generated a veritable mountain of information on social and economic conditions, the bulk of it never before collected or convincingly catalogued. Pittsburgh surveyors reported findings from what today would surely be praised as a rare endeavor in multilevel, multidisciplinary research. It combined fieldwork in Pittsburgh's working-class neighborhoods and steel plants; statistical data collection on wages, hours, working conditions, household budgets, public health and child welfare; personal interviews; analyses of an enormous variety of industry, local government, social agency, church and mutual aid society records; and statistical and observational surveys of environmental indicators ranging from smoke to sewage to recreational space. Its samples of wage-earning Pittsburgh, albeit not statistically representative (few surveys were at the time), included native-born whites, immigrants, and African Americans. All told, the research involved some seventy social scientists, statisticians, engineers, social agency and community volunteers, and—in a stroke of genius that also grew out of the still emerging visual culture of progressive reform—the sketches of artist Joseph Stella and then-amateur photographer Lewis Hine. Paul Kellogg moved to Pittsburgh and established an office with a small staff to oversee the project and manage its several components. At its core, though, was a small group of young, mostly young women, investigators who conducted extended in-depth research and provided the survey with its central focus: Elizabeth Beardsley Butler, assistant secretary of the Consumers' League of New Jersey and author of several studies on women's work; Margaret Byington, a Charity Organization field worker who would later join the RSF staff; Crystal Eastman, then a recent law graduate who would go on to become a leading advocate of workers' compensation and feminist politics; and John A. Fitch, a graduate student of John R. Commons who would base his dissertation on his research for the survey.[14] Their more extensive and scholarly investigations were published by the foundation, in four heavily documented and richly illustrated monographs that would later be supplemented by volumes of previously published articles, essays, brief personal memoirs, and photographs that Kellogg collected and edited under the titles *Wage Earning Pittsburgh* and *The Civic Frontage* (1914).

Each of the monographs would have a career in its own right, in the scholarly literature and in the work of reform. In *The Steel Workers,* published in 1910, John Fitch wrote about the appalling working conditions and authoritarian management practices in the steel mills, portraying workers as physically depleted and powerless, without union representation, to garner a fair share of the enormous profits generated from the low wages, twelve-hour days, seven-day work weeks, and relentlessly sped up production practices they endured. Especially appalling to Fitch, as to the other survey investigators, were the extraordinary lengths to which the U.S. Steel Corporation had gone, which included the use of security enforcement and spies, to repress any possibility of organizing for fair wages, steady advancement, better working conditions, or even free expression in the workplace. Fitch complemented his reporting from the dehumanizing machinations of the factory floor by emphasizing the integrity and humanity of the workers (see figure 1.2).

> To know these men you must see them at work; you must
> stand beside the open-hearth helper as he taps fifty tons of the
> molten steel for his furnace, you must feel the heat of the Besse-
> mer converters as you watch the vesselmen and the steel
> pourer, and above the crash and roar of the booming mills you
> must talk with rollers and hookers, while five and ten-ton steel
> ingots plunge madly back and forth between the rolls. . . . But
> to know them best you should see them at home. There the
> muscular feats of the heater's helper and the rough orders of
> the furnace boss are alike forgotten, and you find a kindly,
> open-hearted, human sort of men.
> —John Andrews Fitch, "Some Pittsburgh Steel Workers"[15]

In *Homestead: The Households of a Mill Town*, also published in
1910, Margaret Byington made the contrast even sharper, by showing how the conditions, rules, and wages set by the corporation extended into the deepest reaches of family and home life and, as con-
veyed so incisively by Hine's photographs, into the lives of future
generations. Drawing on a combination of ethnographic fieldwork
and detailed household budget surveys, Byington documented the
consequences of getting by on less than a living wage and with little control over working conditions. But she also extended her
analysis to the next, community level, where the disparities between corporation and worker, and their consequences, were literally inscribed in the widely disparate neighborhood conditions,
services, educational systems, and tax burdens of Homestead's
three separately incorporated boroughs. These were reflected most
starkly in the contrast between wealthy Munhall, home to the steel
mill and better appointed company housing, and deeply impoverished Homestead proper, where the majority of workers lived and
paid twice the property tax rates of their wealthy neighbors. The
company, Byington concluded, based on detailed fiscal analysis by
fellow surveyor Shelby Harrison (future director of RSF's Surveys
and Exhibits Department) had effectively freed itself from "much
of its local responsibility as a property holder," leaving the resi-
dents of Homestead to "build and maintain schools and public
works, protect person and property, and support local government" (see figure 1.3).[16]

Figure 1.2   Immigrant Day Laborers on the Way Home from
Work, 1907/1908

Source: Photographed by Lewis W. Hine (Fitch 1910, facing p. 145).

It is through the households themselves that the industrial situation impresses itself indelibly upon the life of the people.
The environment of the home afforded by this checkerboard
town tilted on the slope back of the mill site, the smoke which
pours its depressing fumes to add their extra burden to the
housewife's task, the constant interference with orderly routine
due to the irregular succession of long hours—these are the
outward and visible signs of the subordination of household
life to industrial life. The mill affects the family even more inti-
mately through the wage scale to which the standards of home
making, housekeeping, and child rearing must conform. Here
the impressions gained by a season's residence in Homestead
are supported by the budget study of ninety families. For whatever may be the triumph or failure of the steel plant as a man-
ufactory, it must also be judged by the part it has borne in help-

Figure 1.3   In Carnegie's Footsteps

Source: Photographed by Lewis W. Hine (Byington 1910, facing p. 110).

ing or hindering this town, which has grown up on the farm land at the river bend, in becoming a sound member of the American commonwealth.
—Margaret Byington, *Homestead*[17]

Crystal Eastman was even more explicit about drawing a link between workplace conditions—in this case, in the coal mining and railroad as well as the steel industry—and broader public responsibility. Her pioneering research in *Work Accidents and the Law* (1910) provided systematic evidence that the overwhelming burden of workplace accidents fell on working families and communities, despite a preponderance of safety hazards and managerial neglect. For Eastman, however, those consequences, again depicted in photographs and personal interviews as well as in detailed statistical tables, raised questions that went beyond corporate behavior to

Figure 1.4   One Arm and Four Children

Source: Photographed by Lewis W. Hine (Eastman 1910, facing p. 157).

whether and how society understood the broader social value of work and the issues of just compensation and protection from hazard (see figure 1.4). The issue for her was not simply corporate neglect, then, though that was considerable, but also a legal and policy environment that failed utterly to hold corporations responsible for their actions and left the burden on already underpaid workers instead.

> A special cloud always threatens the home of the worker in dangerous trades, because his daily work involves physical risk to him, and on his life and strength depend the happiness of his family. What is his "work" then? Is it any concern of society? First of all, to be sure, it is his way of making a living, but

it is also necessary to his employer's way of making a living, and finally it is necessary to society's way of making a living. If in many fundamental operations of this undertaking there is constant danger to life and limb, it is not just that those whose lot falls in this part of the work should endure not only all the physical torture that comes with injury, but also almost the entire economic loss which inevitably follows it. It is not just that the wives and children, mothers and fathers, of those who do this part of the work, should not only bear the constant dread, the shock, the grief and longing, but also pay in their own harder struggles, and lesser opportunities and narrowed lives, the money-cost of the tragedy. The physical suffering of the injured we cannot share. We cannot satisfy the longing or lessen the grief. But the economic loss we can share. Our failure to do this is an injustice to the wage-earner; and the outcome of this injustice is misery.
—Crystal Eastman, *Work-Accidents and the Law*[18]

Yet it was the first of the survey volumes to be published, Elizabeth Beardsley Butler's *Women and the Trades* (1909a), that would most fully challenge readers to think differently about the meaning and value of industrial work. Based on extraordinarily thorough, in-depth research on the small manufactories, service industries, food processing plants and light industries that barely registered on Steeltown's radar screen, Butler brought complexity to the overwhelmingly male breadwinner image of the industrial workforce—an image other survey volumes reinforced. The working women of Pittsburgh were not only in the industrial workforce to stay; they occupied a uniquely segmented part of the labor force that otherwise remained invisible, much like the vital income they provided for the wage earning household (see figure 1.5).

It requires a moment's readjustment of our angle of vision to see Pittsburgh as a city of working women. To dig crude ores, to fuse and forge them, are not among the lighter handicrafts at which women can readily be employed. The old cry of the dwarfs under the earth, the first metal smiths, rings out in Pitts-

Figure 1.5   Bottling Olives with a Grooved Stick

Source: Photographed by Lewis W. Hine (Butler 1909a, facing p. 41).

burgh in the tap of the minder's tools and in the shouts of gangs of furnacemen and engine crews in the winding recesses of the mill.

Yet even in a city whose prosperity is founded in steel and

coal, there has come into being beside the men a group of co laborers. If we listen again, we hear the cry of the dwarfs (the
productive forces of the earth) not only in the shouts of gangs
of furnacemen, but from the mobile group of workers at the
screw and bolt works, and among the strong-armed women
who make the sandcores in rooms planned like Alberich's
smithy in the underworld. Listen still more closely, and we
hear the dwarf voices in the hum of the machines in a garment
factory, in the steady turn of metal rolls in a laundry, and even
in the clip of the stogy roller's knife in the tiny workroom of a
tenement loft. Side by side with the men, the women workers
have found a place in the industry of the steel district in the Al-
leghenies.

—Elizabeth Beardsley Butler, "The Working Women of
Pittsburgh"[19]

Significant as the volumes were on their own, the real power of
the Pittsburgh Survey was in the larger story it told and the collective portrait it offered. This encompassed life, work, need, opportunity, and hardship in a city that, though long given over to the
rhythms and vicissitudes of industrial steel production, had been
further transformed by the breathtaking concentration and consolidation of power within the industry, the rapid reorganization of
the workplace and hence of family life, and the erosion of opportunity, freedom, and political voice—democracy—as a result. The
corporate restructuring of capitalism and of society was the essential historical backdrop for the survey monographs, brought home
by the living memory of the bloody Homestead strike of 1892, in
which Andrew Carnegie had infamously broken the union, and the
subsequent consolidation of the steel trust in J. P. Morgan's U.S.
Steel Corporation. It was the backdrop for viewing the significance
of the other transformations the survey tracked—Pittsburgh's ongoing urbanization, the environmental degradation, the hardening
class divisions, and the impact of continuing waves of immigrants
from eastern and southern Europe, and to a lesser degree of African
American migrants from the American South.

These structural transformations gave the survey its central narrative. But it was the lives of the wage earners that provided the

lens through which Kellogg and his associates aimed, quite literally and consciously, to reformulate and repicture the social question—or, really, a whole series of compartmentalized social questions—within an analytic framework that would emphasize the interrelationships among them and the need for planned, deliberative public action. For this, Kellogg and his colleagues relied on the most up-to-date methods and technologies of objective inquiry and visual display, from the original "Scheme of the Pittsburgh Survey" (see figure 1.1) to Hine's self-consciously sociological photography, to an extraordinarily comprehensive array of maps, tables, graphs, and images designed for public exhibits and civic deliberation. The role of knowledge so gained and presented would be active and transformative, enabling the community to see what the increasing compartmentalization of modern life obscured—on the one hand, what was genuinely shared and public about its problems, and thus amenable to public and democratic action; on the other, what those problems, and the broader public interest looked like when viewed from the perspective of the wage-earning majority.

What the survey's reform vision did not lead to was the kind of community-based mobilization and consensus-building that Kellogg, at his most ambitious, might have imagined research could inspire. Save for some significant yet limited concessions from the steel corporations and in public health, the surveyors could point to few examples of immediate concrete effects. In a sense, though, the survey's inability to launch a local reform movement misses its larger significance, in terms of its own ambition as well as in the wider tradition of socially purposive research. There the survey did have what Florence Kelley referred to as a rather remarkable chain effect that would ripple through research, reform, and policy circles for decades to come. Prominent among them were such immediate legislative reform connections as that between Crystal Eastman's study and the drive for workers' compensation. The Pittsburgh Survey would also be widely cited in legislative and less formal efforts to regulate hours, wages, and the workweek—efforts that would occupy activists for decades to come. Its impact would also be felt in the widely imitated approach to social investigation it inspired and in the extraordinary networks of research and reform activism it helped to launch—networks and research sensibilities that would be sustained through the efforts of RSF, among others, and that would eventually become an integral part of New Deal reform and administrative culture.[20] Finally, it played an important role in widening and sustaining the effort to use research as a vehicle for promoting a broader social scientific literacy in the democratic public sphere. This was the mission to which the journal that in 1909 became known as *The Survey*, the successor to *Charities and the Commons*, and under Kellogg's editorship, would dedicate itself for the next several decades.

Nowhere was the chain effect of the Pittsburgh Survey more apparent than in the Russell Sage Foundation, which more than any single institution created the space for an ongoing, open-ended reform conversation that aimed—albeit not without internal tensions—to represent a broadly public interest "that would reflect the 95 percent who do not receive a college education."[21]

Research soon became the leading edge of the reform agenda in three areas for which the foundation would gain most renown. In each, research generated within a normative, reformist framework was not necessarily less scientific or objective than its more academic counterparts. If anything, one could argue that reform was more generative of research, in that reform purposes generated the questions that drew social investigators into aspects of urbanization, social relations, and, especially, political economy that were otherwise not being addressed and were not well understood.

One was the decades-long campaign to reform the small loan industry, a campaign that would lead RSF from its war on loan sharks in the early 1910s to a broader emphasis on documenting, regulating and democratizing access to consumer credit from the late 1920s through the mid 1940s—all in the interest, as the foundation saw it, of small debtors and "families of limited means."[22] It would also engage RSF staff in an unusually direct and proactive role in industry and legislative politics. Arthur Ham, the graduate student and later Treasury Department official who directed RSF's Remedial Loans Department from 1910 to 1917, was a tireless publicist, lobbyist, and model legislation drafter in what would eventually become a largely successful nationwide effort to pass state uniform small loan laws, thus laying the groundwork for a legitimate, regulated commercial market as well as for the expansion of new instruments such as credit unions. The effort continued under the "fighting and colorful leadership" of Ham's successor, the economist and (later) New Deal Brain Truster Leon Henderson, who until 1934 headed the foundation's by then renamed Department of Consumer Credit. Subsequently, the directorship was taken over by Henderson's assistant Rolf Nugent, who during the course of his career at the foundation had become one of the country's foremost experts on consumer debt. Small loan legislation had passed in a total of thirty-four states by the mid-1940s, due in no small part to the advice, expert testimony, and the kind of unofficial imprimatur RSF provided.[23]

But the contribution of the foundation's consumer credit department reached well beyond the movement for institutional innovation and legislative reform in the lending industry. It was also significant in providing the research base for what was then emerging as a new, more Keynesian understanding of the role of consumer credit in a changing political economy. During the course of its decades-long campaign, the RSF had established itself as a leading center of empirical research expertise in a field that, with few exceptions, had largely been neglected by academic economists. Thus, for all the reformist zeal with which they first set out to expose the nefarious ways of loan sharks, Arthur Ham and his associates were aware that they were in some senses inventing a research field. They were also meticulous about gathering and appending their reports with an expanding array of data, even when those data were based on decidedly unconventional underground economy research. In this, they were motivated as much by the awareness that empirical documentation would be critical in establishing their credibility as disinterested voices in an intensely heated reform debate. Nevertheless, these early studies documenting the practices of a wide range of quasi-legal and underground lenders would in turn lay essential groundwork for systematic investigations into the newly recognized field of consumer credit. By the end of the 1920s, and with growing urgency as the full weight of the

Great Depression set in, RSF experts were drawing on extensive research and experience from years of reform work for groundbreaking studies of consumer credit, debt, and their growing significance in the economy. This work culminated in Nugent's *Consumer Credit and Economic Stability* (1939), a definitive text that drew recognition for its detailed documentation of the sources and uses of consumer credit but also for drawing on Keynesian theory to understand its critical role in generating and sustaining economic demand. Nugent would go on to apply his expertise at some of the major administrative outposts of the new economic thinking, the Office of Price Administration, and, later in overseas development work for the United Nations.

What was reflected, then, in RSF's shift from calling its department remedial loans to calling it consumer credit was far more than a change of nomenclature and far more than two decades of accumulated expertise. There was a general shift in economic perspective and an embrace of Keynes. Along with the Twentieth Century Fund, RSF had become a site of economic and policy learning that would later be reflected in the New Deal. Equally important was the profoundly shifting normative framework that accompanied RSF's reform work, and to which Henderson and Nugent both contributed. This shift, from an early emphasis on encouraging working-class savings and thrift to recognizing and protecting working-class consumer rights indicated a new, more expansive idea of economic citizenship that would find its fullest expression in the Office of Price Administration and in Franklin Delano Roosevelt's promise—however partial—of "freedom from want."[24] Reform, then, was a venue for new ways of documenting and thinking about the economy and the tools of economic policy. Henderson, as a chief Office of Price Administration official, became a renowned and influential advocate of consumer rights, wage standards, and price controls.[25]

Research also played a central role in a second of RSF's reform objectives: transforming the broadly encompassing field known as charity organization into modernized social scientific philanthropy. Of course, the notion of making charity more scientific was not in and of itself new. But where scientific charity had been about intel-

40

ligent almsgiving, friendly visiting, and distinguishing between the deserving and the undeserving poor, social scientific philanthropy would be about improving professional social work practices, and attacking poverty rather than merely uplifting the poor. Here the foundation weighed in not only to promote efficiency and professionalism in how charity and social work were administered but also, in the aftermath of the bruising battles over New York's repeal of welfare in the 1890s, to make underlying social conditions rather than individual pauperism the target of charitable investigation and intervention.

That there was an underlying, though not sharply divisive, tension between these aims was evident in the division of labor between casework and more broadly social investigation institutionalized at RSF and reflective of tensions in the field writ large. Under the direction of social work leader Mary Richmond, the foundation's Department of Charity Organization would remain focused on perfecting the techniques and establishing scientific standards for what Richmond, as the author of the field's leading textbook, dubbed *Social Diagnosis* (1917). Those standards, as set forth in Richmond's writings and institutionalized in RSF-funded schools of social welfare, prompted social workers to view their clients within a more clinical mental health and socially environmental framework while maintaining a focus on individual and family casework techniques. In various departments and in long-term research on urban social conditions, however, RSF would adopt a less individualized and personally prescriptive reform vision, built from knowledge about social and structural conditions in housing, poverty, and public health. Here the interests of reform drew the foundation into the more wide-ranging, transatlantic social policy conversation that focused on ideas about social insurance, housing reform, urban planning, workplace protection, and unemployment policy that would translate broad concerns about the social question into concrete programs of research and reform.[26]

Nowhere would reform translate more fully into a program of social scientific research than in the area Mary van Kleeck headed for nearly forty years starting in 1910, save for a brief interval as director of the U.S. Labor Department's Women in Industry Service

41

and to lay the institutional groundwork for the U.S. Women's Bureau from 1917 to 1919. Like so many other women and men of her generation, van Kleeck came to the still-forming professions of social science and philanthropy as a young college graduate and settlement house affiliate. The latter yielded hands-on field experience as a researcher in the factories and child labor mills of New York City. She began her long career at RSF running its Committee on Women's Work, which itself had a stated interest in improving conditions through protective legislation, public pressure, and more enlightened, efficient management. The aim of research was in this sense to lay a factual basis for reform. But it was also more broadly aimed at educating, shaping, and disabusing public opinion of its stubborn conventions. Thus would van Kleeck's RSF program—and, later, the U.S. Women's Bureau she had helped to launch—emphasize what mainstream public opinion continued to resist. Women were a growing, permanent, and legitimate part of the industrial workforce, with rights to training, fair wages, and the full benefits of economic citizenship, as well as special protection from exploitative working conditions.[27]

Within a few years, van Kleeck's Committee on Women's Work had been upgraded to a research division, and had built up an extraordinarily impressive record, with detailed, extensively documented studies of women in a number of industries chosen as much for their strategic reform as for their research interests. Thus, for example, major RSF studies focused on women in bookbinding—the test case in ongoing court contests over the constitutionality of New York laws restricting night work—and artificial flower-making, long a target of activist organizations such as the National Consumers' League due to its heavy reliance on exploitative tenement-based home work. Although centrally focused on industrial work, van Kleeck's division did not confine its inquiries to what happened on the job. A major study of Italian working-class women—among the most exploited and vilified of New York's new immigrant population—was based on extensive, neighborhood-based research conducted with the help of an Italian-speaking resident, and emphasized the degree to which "women's work"—from household, to factory, to community and back—was, literally, never done.[28] Findings from these and other studies produced several books, but were even more consciously reported in the periodicals, pamphlets, and popular journals that found wider public circulation and in progressive labor and social policy reform circles. Soon, RSF could link its research to a number of practical outcomes, including citations in renowned Brandeis briefs successfully arguing for the constitutionality of protective labor legislation for women, as well as to legislative debates over hours and workplace regulation. Alongside the Women's Bureau, van Kleeck's department became a leading center for expertise on a subject that had been largely marginalized in academic economics circles.[29] Notably, in the course of building this research division, van Kleeck trained a number of social work graduate students in fieldwork; she also honed research methods that had been built up within the settlement house and public agency inquiries as well, of course, as in the Pittsburgh Survey itself. All research projects involved fieldwork and direct contact with workers as well as collection of statistical data on wages, hours, and working conditions—some of it drawn from reluctantly opened company records, and under the threat of company re-prisal. On more than one occasion, RSF officials intervened to protect van Kleeck and her department from such threats.[30]

For van Kleeck, though, these intensively empirical studies were increasingly of interest for larger purposes of economic research, policy, and reform. Even as she was about to enter war service as head of the Women in Industry Service, she was beginning to steer RSF research to focus on issues of concern to working men as well as women, and to illuminate the rapidly changing landscape of industrial work, the broader economic problems of unemployment, worker health, household standards of living, and the perennial labor question. Under the expanded purview of the RSF's Department of Industrial Studies, van Kleeck developed an increasingly wide-ranging and internationalized body of economic and policy research. Throughout, she positioned the foundation as a source of accurate, disinterested expertise, generated in response to unfolding problems and detached from any single economic theory or reform. Its objective was "not in defense of any one program of reform, nor as a contribution to economic theory. . . but rather in the

43

faith that the community itself must discover its own program of action and that common knowledge is the foundation of wise public opinion."[31] In fact, that stance hardly captured the intellectual scope or political ambition of the program. Van Kleeck's contribution would be in more actively shaping and fleshing out the boundaries of the progressive-labor-social democratic conversation with a research agenda that first looked to the promises of cooperative, scientific management and eventually to more nationalized, state-centered social and economic planning in search of a program that would reconcile the goals of increased productivity and labor democracy.

These combined commitments were reflected in van Kleeck's ongoing work on unemployment statistics, but most clearly in a unique series of studies published as part of a program in industrial relations. Launched amidst heightened fears of unemployment, labor strife, and trade union radicalism after World War I, the series was set up to document and evaluate five prominent experiments in labor management cooperation. Significantly, the first of these drew van Kleeck's research division head to head with a philanthropic rival. The study was of the Rockefeller Plan of employee representation that had been instituted by the Rockefeller-controlled Colorado Fuel and Iron Company in the wake of the coal miners' strike of 1913, a strike that turned deadly for workers and their families when the company brought in the state militia. The plan itself—and, because it grew out of a foundation grant, the Rockefeller philanthropies as well—had been roundly denounced as an effort to whitewash the company and the Standard Oil Trust. The RSF study, authored by staff member Ben Selekman and published despite Rockefeller's objections, was more measured in its extensively researched documented assessment, reporting the Rockefeller Plan to be incomplete as a scheme for genuine worker participation.[32] Subsequent case studies in the series found examples of company-based agreements that "worked," the most expansive among them giving workers a voice in management, a share in profits, and rewards for the increased efficiency improved relations produced.[33]

By the 1930s and the early New Deal, however, van Kleeck

was increasingly convinced that such cooperative arrangements, though possible and in some cases highly productive, simply would not be widely adopted on a voluntary basis, and indeed were being undermined by the fiercely competitive principles of unplanned American capitalism. She was also convinced that the voluntaristic, National Recovery Administration (NRA) approach to industrial relations was wholly inadequate—a conviction she shared with a great many others, including her former colleague Leon Henderson, in the progressive-labor coalition. Van Kleeck, however, chose to make the conviction public in a pamphlet announcing her resignation from the NRA advisory board after only one day of serving.[34] She would continue to be assertive about her growing radicalism throughout the Great Depression and postwar years, moving from the statist social democratic left to unapologetic support for Soviet-style planning well after revelations about the Stalinist purges and totalitarian nature of that regime. Van Kleeck was also extraordinarily active and highly visible in international policy and reform circles. For all this, she would be aggressively red-baited in the 1940s and in a series of McCarthyite investigations of foundations in the 1950s, by which time she had been retired, her program ended in the foundation reorganization of the late 1940s. And yet, during an earlier time, when the reform conversation was much broader in scope and less constricted by cold war anticommunism, van Kleeck maintained a firm and prominent place at the RSF, as she did within the world of economic and policy research, despite her increasingly controversial politics. Along with John Glenn and Shelby Harrison, she was by far the most visible member of the RSF staff. Notably, when RSF trustees began in the 1930s to put disclaimers on van Kleeck's RSF-published work, they indicated approval of the empirical methods but distanced themselves from her more radical conclusions.

The last major book in the Industrial Relations series, *Miners and Management*, a highly favorable study of the Rocky Mountain Fuel Company's agreement with the United Mine Workers, written by van Kleeck and published in 1934, offers some hint of how van Kleeck negotiated the conflicting pulls of empiricism and radical politics. Her empirical findings led her to conclude that the agreement had been a substantial success, based on extensively documented evidence of worker satisfaction, increased productivity, and employment stability. In a separate conclusion, however, she argued that despite the success of this cooperative agreement the notoriously cutthroat coal industry should be socialized outright in the interest not only of dealing with the crisis of the Great Depression, but also of giving workers a greater voice in a democratically planned economy.[35] Van Kleeck based this conclusion on the combination of her own shifting reform politics and a much longer experience with industrial research. What is more significant, however, is the way she turned this apparent success story into an argument for much more sweeping reform: not at all by subordinating her findings to existing commitments but by providing evidence that the Rocky Mountain Fuel Company was the exception to the rule.

Clearly, the early RSF was far more than the social work–oriented Charity Trust of reputation. Although key programs remained anchored in charity organization and social work, the foundation was also a diversified social and economic research institution that, in its combination of applied and, increasingly, basic research, was itself an ongoing experiment in social and policy relevance. Nor can it easily be described as a think tank in what has come, until recently, to be the accepted meaning of that term.[36] For, contrary to the encapsulated, socially remote neutrality suggested by the image, the RSF was unapologetically part of a diversified reform culture that, though hardly dormant in the 1920s, found its energies vastly renewed and refocused by the challenges of worldwide depression and the political opening for social scientific activism in Franklin Delano Roosevelt's New Deal and World War II. It was as part of that culture that key figures at RSF used knowledge not simply to report the facts but as well to grab hold of and continually to find new ways of engaging the variegated and changing social question, and to expand the boundaries of the policy conversation well beyond the confines of either laissez faire or Herbert Hoover's associationalism. That Mary van Kleeck, the Pittsburgh surveyors, and a host of other RSF investigators did so within an institution that owed its existence to, remained firmly committed to, and looked for trusteeship to leading figures of industrial capitalism and charity organization speaks less to their status as renegades than to the open-ended nature of their commitment to a "social point of view" concerned principally with the "welfare of the less favorably situated groups in society."[37] It was also as part of that purposive reform culture that RSF established a separate Bureau of Information, issued its research findings in hundreds of pamphlets, and continued to subsidize the *Survey* and *Survey Graphic*. Connection to that reform network is what made the research relevant, effective, and designed to engage not just with powerful established officials but also with a far broader public for which knowing about its problems would be a vital part of finding democratic solutions.

There were limitations and blind spots, to be sure, in RSF's "social science in the making," and few more glaring than the failure, as one of the country's leading philanthropic reform organizations, to take up directly or to engage the race question in any sustained or meaningful way. There was also a point beyond which the broadly defined survey tradition, with its largely atheoretical and inductive method, simply could not go in the search for deeper explanations for enduring social questions and for new ways of achieving society's highest ideals. As I discuss in chapter 2, it was in the effort to deepen and extend the progressive knowledge tradition in precisely those ways that the scholars would turn the social question on social science itself.

◈ CHAPTER 2 ◈

SOCIAL SCIENCE, THE SOCIAL QUESTION, AND THE VALUE-NEUTRALITY DEBATE

When RSF reinvented itself as a social science foundation in the late 1940s, it did not simply break with an earlier vision of social scientific reform. Its trustees also embraced an alternative and, in its own way, equally value-laden vision of relevant social science that had been honed and institutionalized with increasing momentum since the 1920s—in research universities, in professional societies, in an expanding nonprofit research sector, and in a philanthropic politics of knowledge that, though by no means wholly absent from the early RSF, was most closely associated with the Carnegie Corporation and the Rockefeller Foundation's Laura Spelman Rockefeller Memorial Fund.[1]

That vision, of a neutral, politically detached, and more academically grounded and "scientistic" social science, did not originate with the major foundations. It did, however, become the program of the two biggest and leading social science funders, and through them of an officially nonideological, incrementalist, and managerial reformism that ratified the basic outlines of the corporate-government-academic alliance envisioned in Herbert Hoover's associative state.[2] The foundations in turn played a central role in institutionalizing the idea of neutrality as the basis of social scientific relevance and expertise. They did so with massive infusions of support for such leading centers of academic social science as the University of Chicago and Columbia, and in newly established

48

nonprofit organizations such as the National Bureau of Economic Research (NBER, founded in 1920), the Social Science Research Council (SSRC, created in 1923), and the Brookings Institution (created out of the merger of nominally separate institutes of government and economics in 1927).[3] With foundation money, close ties to business and government, and often overlapping networks of academics and boards of trustees, these organizations became the standard-bearers for what constituted neutral expertise in the independent—which is to say, nongovernmental and nonprofit—research sector. It was to these institutions that Herbert Hoover would turn throughout the 1920s as sources of knowledge on a wide range of economic and administrative issues, and, on the eve of a Great Depression that Hoover's experts failed to forecast, for the latest in social scientific thinking about the major social developments that would challenge American society in the coming decade. The result, *Recent Social Trends*, was indeed a comprehensive and authoritative survey that synthesized a tremendous amount and range of social research. It also captured something significant in its deliberately neutered tone. By the time the massive study was published in 1934, the social question loomed larger than ever, but its essential character, as framed by the social scientific experts, had changed. The problems presented by recent social trends—admittedly massive problems involving governance, democracy, political economy, the family, the physical environment, and more—were best stated as problems of social (im)balance, (dis)equilibrium, and (mal)adjustment. In reporting them, the task of social science was strictly technical, requiring the authors to refrain from expressing opinions and instead to focus on providing officials with information for more efficient planning.[4]

At the time, though, and throughout the interwar years, this vision of value-neutral social science, albeit increasingly dominant and favored in official circles, was still very much in play.[5] For one thing, neutrality became institutionalized as a sort of semiofficial knowledge standard within a much broader and highly politicized context of knowledge mobilization and proliferating expertise, in which activist organizations—partly in response to diminished opportunities for political mobilization by other means, but also in recognition of the growing political salience of organized knowledge—created or greatly expanded their research capacities.[6] Although this broader institutionalization of knowledge occurred across the political spectrum, it was especially vigorous in leading labor and such prominent progressive reform organizations as the National Consumers' League, the National Urban League, and the social insurance–oriented American Association for Labor Legislation. Along with the Russell Sage Foundation, this segment of the expanding nongovernmental research and advocacy sector maintained a robust tradition of reform-oriented social scientific research. Alternatives to neutrality could also be found in academe, notably in the heavily applied and policy-oriented brand of institutionalist economics practiced by John R. Commons and others at the University of Wisconsin, Madison, and in the high-powered collection of radical and left-leaning interracialist black scholars (E. Franklin Frazier and Ralph Bunche prominent among them) in the social sciences at Howard University.

Moreover, and especially significant for this discussion, even as it gained in prestige and institutional power, the ideal of neutral objectivity was subject to ongoing debate—often heated, and often from within the very organizations established to uphold the highest standards of professional social scientific integrity. In the 1930s and 1940s, amidst the crises of worldwide economic depression and impending war, these debates famously broke out into the broader public sphere—first in the sociologist Robert S. Lynd's critique of what he considered to be an overly technical, narrowly empiricist social science, *Knowledge for What* (1939), and soon thereafter in Gunnar Myrdal's vast, synthesizing reframing of what was then called the Negro Problem, *An American Dilemma* (1944). Together, these critiques and the broader discussions they provoked crystallized a challenge to the viability of neutral social science as a scientific ideal, as a strategy for engaging public issues, and especially as a way of conceptualizing the role of knowledge at a time when liberal democracy was imperiled by mass unemployment, racial inequality, and the rise of political authoritarianism.

A great deal has changed since Lynd and Myrdal issued their challenges. Social science has grown far more diverse and more self-critical—more aware, due in part to the influence of postmodern criticisms, of the constructed nature of social knowledge. Subsequent critics, usually writing from disciplinary perspectives, have continually returned to the themes Lynd and Myrdal raised—of crisis, relevance, commitment, and the (im)possibility of scientific objectivity in social knowledge, addressing them in more contemporary if not necessarily more sophisticated ways.[7] Indeed, viewed through the sensibilities of a later, more postmodern generation, aspects of what Lynd and Myrdal had to say may seem old-fashioned or commonplace. Among other things, they are largely innocent of what feminist and postmodern critics in particular have told us about the hidden inequities and biases that are replicated in empirical research models.[8]

Still, Lynd and Myrdal remain important touchstones for the ongoing debate about values and neutrality in social science and are especially relevant to that question as social science confronts it today. One reason is that they represent and connect the conversation to a long established, still vital, but never dominant thread within professional social science that challenges the neutral or value-free ideal from within the empirical research tradition. Although often writing from its very edges, Lynd, Myrdal, and others, such as the sociologist C. Wright Mills, continued to grapple with the question of whether and how social science could be an active part of working toward a democratic polity and culture while also working within empirical research norms.[9] At the same time, as intellectuals who early in their careers had been engaged in social gospel and reform work, they remained part of the socially normative research tradition even as they looked to a more academic and theoretical inquiry to get beyond its heavily empirical emphasis. In this, they suggest an enduring intellectual and purposive link between social science and social scientific reform. This was a link that the Russell Sage Foundation would aim to maintain after it changed direction in 1947, albeit in a much different way, with a program to train social workers (and other professionals) in social scientific theory and methods.

A second reason for their enduring relevance is that in raising the question of democratic values and the role of social scientific research they addressed their criticisms not only to social science but also to the broader culture. The impact of their scholarship would be felt at least as much if not more in popular and political than in academic culture. For this impact, as for their political leanings, Lynd and Myrdal became fodder in that segment of the long post-war culture war that would, as I discuss in chapter 3, focus on social scientific knowledge and lead to the rise of a new, explicitly conservative knowledge and policy establishment.

Last, Lynd and Myrdal were quite self-consciously writing at a moment when not only questions about social science but also the larger social question was deeply contested, such that it could not, they believed, be engaged within a strictly neutral or value-free social scientific frame. So Lynd and Myrdal present us with a parallel, however imperfect, to our own historical moment, when the limits of neutral social knowledge are stretched by the challenges of inequality and ideology.

Constructing Neutrality

In light of the shift from reform to neutrality, it is no small irony that the philanthropic turn to a neutral social science was initially hastened not by fear of "radical" associations, but by controversies over "tainted wealth." Such suspicions had been raised from the start of the gigantic philanthropic enterprise that created the Russell Sage, Carnegie, and Rockefeller foundations between 1907 and 1913. But the link between foundation-sponsored research and capitalist intrigue—a corporate plot to "control the education and 'social service' of the nation," in the words of one prominent critic—reached sensational heights with the investigations of the congressionally chartered Commission on Industrial Relations in 1914 and 1915.[10]

Chartered in 1912, with endorsements from long-time RSF executive director John Glenn as well as a number of liberal businessmen, to find solutions to the virtual warfare between capital and labor then gripping the nation, the decidedly pro-labor commission combined labor market research with a series of high-profile hearings and site visits to the bloodiest battlefields of the day.[11] None drew more attention than the Ludlow Massacre, which left fifty-three striking miners, including two women and eleven children, dead at Rockefeller's Colorado Fuel and Iron Company. It led eventually to the Rockefeller Plan that Mary van Kleeck's department made part of its industrial relations series. Enraged at John D. Rockefeller Jr.'s efforts to acquit the family with a foundation-sponsored study of industrial relations (among other more obvious public relations measures), Commission Chairman Frank P. Walsh turned his subpoena power on the whole of philanthropy, but on Rockefeller philanthropy in particular. In hearings and public statements that would cause even Paul Kellogg, then editor of the *Survey*, to come to the foundation's defense, Walsh accused Rockefeller of using the vast profits from exploited labor to "exact a tribute of loyalty and subserviency to him and his interest from a whole profession of scientists, social workers and economists."[12] Recommendations from the deeply divided commission notwithstanding, Congress refused to institute significant regulation of the philanthropic trusts. The Rockefeller Foundation, however, quickly ended its brief foray into industrial relations and any other research that could be construed to engage the foundation too directly with labor or other controversial social and economic questions.

The accusation about tainted wealth, of course, was not what kept officers of the Rockefeller and the Carnegie philanthropies— by far largest sources of philanthropic support for social science at the time—from funding social survey and other research that hewed too closely to industrial reform. After all, as we've seen, association with what Mary van Kleeck called the "benefactions of the rich" did not prevent the RSF from maintaining "its predominantly social point of view" of how industrial relations affected "the welfare of the less favorably situated groups in society."[13] Nor was it simply an effort to avoid controversial issues. When Rockefeller and Carnegie did fund research on controversial social questions, they simply approached indirectly, in what would become standard foundation practice, through the expanding array of intermediary organizations their grants were funding. Far more influential was the basic conservatism of their orientation as philanthropic reformers, and as adherents of that part of the new liberalism—corporate liberalism, as it has come to be known—that associated the common good less with social democracy, labor, and the state than with efficiently managed capitalist markets and sound public administration, and a voluntaristic civil society. Far more influential, too, was the "taint" of progressivism in a political atmosphere of official intolerance for radicalism and dissent.

But philanthropy's embrace of a neutral social science was also rooted in a different, albeit complementary ideology of scientific empiricism, forcefully articulated by a rising generation of social scientific entrepreneurs including the economist Wesley C. Mitchell, the political scientist Robert Merriam, and the sociologists William Ogburn and Robert Park—who were instrumental in founding the core institutions of scientistic social science, and expert at raising foundation funds. Though sharing some of the same characteristic commitments as progressive reform researchers—to rational, scientific inquiry, to empirical methods, to an increased role for knowledge and planning in economic and public affairs— the rising generation of empiricists explicitly rejected the idea that social science should take social betterment as its goal. They were also determined to distinguish themselves from what they considered the intelligent and well-meaning but ultimately limited research of the social survey and settlement house movements, despite having borrowed from their techniques.[14] Few were more outspoken or adamant on the subject than Ogburn, who said in his presidential address to the American Sociological Society that "sociology as a science is not interested in making the world a better place to live."[15] Indeed, social science had no business in social reform. Its mission was to establish the facts objectively and to let those facts speak for themselves. Only on that basis would social science establish its credibility and be of real use to society and to the political leadership it sought to address.[16]

Key to implementing this idea of expert neutrality were a number of developments within academic and professional social science that seemed to bring those softer disciplines closer in line with ideals of objectivity and scientific authority drawn from the natural sciences. One was a growing emphasis on technical and methodological proficiency—especially, though not exclusively, statistical—in the collection and analysis of data. More and better data, in turn, would become the basis for strictly objective research on sub-jects ranging from business cycles to social attitudes. It would also become the focus of institutions such as the National Bureau of Eco-nomic Research, which, under the direction of Wesley Mitchell and in response to the federal decommissioning of temporary statistical agencies after World War I, launched major projects on national in-come and its distribution as it pursued Mitchell's long-term interest in establishing a statistical basis for tracking and explaining busi-ness cycles. Despite the clearly practical nature and potential re-form implications of such research—the income distribution study, for example, documented low working-class standards of living and huge concentrations at the top—Mitchell went to great lengths to keep personal judgment or any semblance of policy recommen-dations out of NBER reports. He also made it a point to put repre-sentatives from labor as well as business on his board of advisers, at least in part to offset pressure from foundation funders.[17] In much the same way, the Social Science Research Council, under the leadership of Charles Merriam and with funding from all the major foundations, positioned itself as a strictly neutral service organiza-tion devoted to better methods—again in the name of bettering so-cial science rather than changing social conditions.

Also contributing to the construction of a neutral social scientific standard was the emergence of theoretical models that made social inquiry more amenable to such scientific methods as hypothesis testing, experimentation, case study, and mathematical analysis—and, in the process, to the scientific values of prediction and control. Social scientists were deeply suspicious of the laissez-faire and So-cial Darwinist doctrines and, increasingly, of the scientific racism that still passed for theory in some quarters. At the same time, from across the new liberal spectrum, they turned to theory to help make sense of, rationalize, and, to varying degrees, exert some control over the direction of social and economic change. Ultimately, even the most stringent of inductive, empirical methodologists had as their aim the development of some kind of predictive theory, even as they pointed to the ascendancy of scientific theory and method as key distinguishing factors between scientific and reform re-search. Equally important, from the standpoint of the foundations, the emergence of a more scientific and theoretical social science offered ostensibly more neutral ways of framing volatile issues in social welfare and political economy.

Robert Park's urban sociology proved especially compelling in this regard. By envisioning a future of racial progress as part of a cycle of contact, conflict, and assimilation without a struggle for rights, it offered a naturalistic model of growth and intergroup relations that pointedly diminished the need for reform. Similarly, problems earlier characterized in the Pittsburgh Survey and elsewhere in terms of the conflict between organized corporate capital and industrial democracy could be explained more benignly as a problem of temporary maladjustment to inevitable, and technology-driven economic modernization in William Ogburn's theory of cultural lag. Thus, in a telling choice of example, Ogburn illustrated his theory using the kinds of workplace accidents Crystal Eastman had studied in Pittsburgh. He explained them as the product of technological advance and the adoption of workers' compensation laws not as a product of political organizing but as part of the necessary adjustment to more efficient modes of production.[18] Cultural lag was even more encompassing as the framework for the Hoover Commission report on *Recent Social Trends*. That report depicted problems ranging from unemployment and crime to rising divorce rates as expressions of "maladjustment" and "uneven development" amidst a chaotic, but ultimately progressive process of modernization.

None had more to offer the search for a theoretically and practically neutral social science, though, than economics. Wesley Mitchell's painstaking statistical research promised someday to provide a broadly institutionalist understanding of the business cycle, at a time when institutionalism was considered the New Economics of the day. Marginalist theory—the leading edge of neoclassical political economy—offered abstract, market-oriented principles for assessing wage standards, in contrast to more overtly moral criteria of fairness and need. In either case, economic theory offered ways of understanding capitalism as a rationalistic if not entirely self-regulating system without retreating into laissez faire. This is not to say that theory itself, or even these particular theories, were inherently conservative. Indeed, there was a parallel theoretical turn in reform circles that would lead figures such as Paul Douglas, economist and later Illinois senator, to use wage theory for both academic and reform purposes, and Robert S. Lynd, as we will see, to put the theory of cultural lag to use in his own social criticism. Nevertheless, the theories that came to dominate the profession and the emerging social science establishment were more likely to have a conservatizing influence in that they stressed naturalistic limits to what policy could do without violating economic or sociological principles.

Reinforcing the academic contribution to more neutral ways of framing social issues was a related trend within major research universities. It was most visible in a series of high-profile academic freedom cases in the 1880s and 1890s, and again during World War I, to restrict overtly political activity and otherwise to punish dissent on the part of faculty.[19] Along with the combined disillusionments of the war and consolidating corporate power, suppression of dissent led to a rechanneling of political activism on the part of a great many intellectuals and academics during the 1920s, toward a politics that emphasized mobilizing scientific expertise and "telling truth to power" over mobilizing the grassroots.[20]

Finally, it is important to underscore that all of these tendencies got a tremendous boost from the patronage of the well-heeled philanthropies and key figures on their boards of trustees and from no less a figure than President Herbert Hoover. Starting with his tenure as secretary of commerce under Presidents Harding and Coolidge, Hoover had been a major proponent of social science as a handmaiden to better government. His efforts to mobilize expertise were especially effective in persuading businessmen of the virtues of scientific data and nonstatist planning. It was above all through this patronage and the institutions it established that neutrality became most fully ensconced in the social scientific and in the broader policy and knowledge establishment it was meant to serve.[21]

The social science that emerged from all this was not so much ideologically neutral as neutralized in several ways. First was in its apolitical way of framing the issues in terms of impersonal processes and inevitable forces rather than struggles over power and control, in its imperative on keeping social scientists insulated from direct political engagement. Second was in the essential conservatism of its commitment to capitalism and its emphasis on service without fundamentally challenging the status quo. Third was in framing its own value commitments as scientific theory and method. Last was in rejecting social betterment as a legitimate object for social science. As social scientific expertise became more institutionalized within official policy circles, it would also become more limited in its idea of the public it was addressing. That is, it would become more focused on a dialogue of experts talking to experts than in reaching and forming a more democratic public. In this way, the emergence of organized expertise represented a neutralized way of exercising power—through knowledge and over knowledge-making—in politics and the public sphere and in the capacity to shape the parameters of policy.

At the same time, though increasingly dominant by virtue of greater resources, the neutralized model of policy relevant social science was by no means exclusive, and by no means the only viable one. As we have seen, the Russell Sage Foundation remained a major funder of objective, reform-minded research and of the community-based survey movement. Efforts to distance themselves notwithstanding, proponents of a more scientistic social science still operated within research and funding networks that overlapped and were very much in conversation with reform research. Mary van Kleeck was among those regularly called on for expertise on unemployment, women and work, and industrial relations. Shelby Harrison, head of the RSF social survey division, and major proponent of the use of surveys for reform purposes, was a member of President Hoover's Commission on Recent Social Trends, as well as of influential SSRC committees. For their part, and especially at a time when avenues for political activism and dissent were more limited, various consumer, labor, and other reform advocates were organizing expertise of their own—aware that to be effective they needed to meet standards of objectivity and accuracy, but nevertheless willing to be explicit about their commitments to reform.

Knowledge for What?

Few figures better capture the ongoing, if contested, dialogue between neutral and normative social science than Robert S. Lynd. Lynd was a Columbia University sociologist, consumer advocate, sometime New Dealer, and co-author with his wife Helen of the best-selling sociological classic *Middletown* (1929). In 1939, he coined what is surely the most widely invoked, if not the most famous, of sociological questions—the social question of social science, if you will—in a book destined to become his second, if lesser known, sociological classic, *Knowledge for What?* In it, he offered a sweeping indictment of a social science in crisis—not, the Great Depression aside, for want of research or even public support, but because of its failure, despite reams of objective data, to answer, or even to explore, as he put it, such fundamental questions as "the intractability of the human factor . . . that has spoiled the American dream." Social science, Lynd thought, had failed to assume the deeper responsibilities of social knowledge to democracy in its own time of crisis. For that, it would have to transcend the boundaries of its safely insulated and neutral stance.[22]

Lynd's entrée into social science was itself the product of the overlapping networks and still-fluid boundaries between social gospel, journalism, academic social science, and reform activism that shaped his own and his generation's approach to social knowledge. It started out in his search for social purpose in the loosely Protestant, ecumenical reform ministry. It proceeded, circuitously, through critical journalism and amateur social investigation to widespread popular recognition and the heights of academic prestige. It was facilitated, again as for so many in his generation, by his encounters with Rockefeller philanthropy.[23]

The initial encounter was hardly auspicious, in that it involved one of John D. Rockefeller Jr.'s more flat-footed efforts to quell controversy over Standard Oil's labor practices with foundation largesse. This time the battlefield was an oil camp in Elk Basin, Wyoming, where Lynd, then a ministry student at Union Theological Seminary, spent the summer of 1922 on missionary assignment.

He was appalled by the impoverished social conditions, lack of union representation, and unnecessarily grueling six-and-a-half day, twelve-hour shift work regime he encountered when he signed on as a roustabout for the local subsidiary of Standard Oil of Indiana. He was also pained by the inadequacy of his rather genteel, book-learned theology to meet the spiritual needs of his would-be congregation, a sentiment captured in his characteristically pithy title for an article published in *Harper's*, "Crude Oil Religion."[24] It was one of two pieces Lynd wrote chronicling his summer ministry. The second, written for the *Survey* and titled "Done in Oil," was more of a journalistic social investigation, illustrated with tables and graphs and evocative photographs of the town, the people, and the oil fields, and heavily documented to expose the huge profits Standard Oil was realizing from the operation—despite Rockefeller's denial of the subsidiary relationship. Faced with Lynd's embarrassingly thorough documentation, Rockefeller at first offered to build a library in Elk Basin in exchange for keeping the still unpublished article under wraps. Lynd declined. Rockefeller then took the high road of a published response in the same issue of *Survey*, a brief mea culpa (of sorts) distancing Standard Oil from direct responsibility but endorsing industry adoption of changes such as the eight-hour workday nonetheless.[25]

By then back in New York, Lynd had decided that his own activist inclinations would be better realized in social science than in ministering the social gospel, and had enrolled for coursework with John Dewey and Wesley Mitchell at Columbia University. He also found gainful employment with another Standard Oil subsidiary, no doubt paying more than his summer wages of $4.05 a day. In a move superficially unlikely but not at all uncommon in philanthropy, the Rockefeller Foundation brought Lynd, one of its most prominent critics, into its circle of grantees, as the principal investigator, joined by Helen Lynd as full coinvestigator, of what was to be a strictly empirical survey of religion in a typical, midsized, midwestern American city.[26] The quite unexpected result, *Middletown*, once again put Lynd at odds with the country's most powerful philanthropist, or at least with the enterprise he spawned. This was not in the least for bringing his own judgments and interpretive frameworks to the study. More significantly, it was for turning the study into an anthropological survey of modern American culture, a culture grounded in the day-to-day rhythms of industrial capitalism (depicted in memorably titled chapters on "The Long Arm of the Job," and "Why Do They Work So Hard?") and wholly given over to the boosterish, business-dominated values of the new consumer economy.

The word anthropological is key here because it captures what distinguished the Lynds as amateur social scientists from their Progressive-era forebears as well as from their more established academic contemporaries. The distinction would also prove critical to Lynd's emerging vision of a social science that was theoretical and empirically objective as well as practical and socially purposeful. It was practical in being grounded in the realities of daily life and actual rather than abstracted human behavior. It was purposeful in illuminating problems otherwise obscured by what Lynds called "the long arm of the job," the "dominance of the dollar," or the "endless stream of new things to buy," and in offering the theoretical apparatus to address them. For this, the Lynds looked beyond the empirical survey and the old social economy to the theoretical tools and methods of the new social anthropology, which provided, as the anthropologist Clark Wissler noted in his foreword, the objectivity and distance of the "outsider," "approaching an American community as one does a primitive tribe."[27] They also borrowed from the social theorist William Ogburn, who would later clash with Robert Lynd at the SSRC, in adapting the theory of cultural lag. Yet the Lynds, with their reform sensibilities intact, used the concept as a tool for reformulating a question akin to that asked in the Pittsburgh Survey. Why was a society committed to the values of small-town communitarianism and participatory democracy complacent amidst the growing disparities of class and power that had become a defining feature of modern life? For the answer, the Lynds looked not to older reform research but to a more deeply analytical, theoretically informed, and still empirical social science. Social science, distinct for the Lynds from atheoretical social investigation, would thus become a tool for asking deeply critical questions about society and its prevailing cultural norms—especially, as they argued in the depression-era follow-up *Middletown in Transition* (1937), for showing how the cultural mythology of free enterprise and laissez faire was thwarting the search for more democratic planning.

If *Middletown*'s critical edge set the Lynds off from more dominant trends and sponsors in the profession, it did not undermine their social scientific careers. In this, the Rockefeller Foundation's refusal to publish the manuscript turned out to be fortuitous. Released to publish the manuscript elsewhere, on the theory that there would be no takers, they found in Harcourt Brace a major commercial publisher with a genius for mass marketing, able to draw a rare combination of popular and academic acclaim for the book.[28] Helen Lynd subsequently joined the faculty of Sarah Lawrence College. Robert, awarded a Ph.D. using the manuscript as his dissertation, was appointed graduate professor of sociology at Columbia in 1931, following a two-year stint at the Social Science Research Council as its executive secretary. Now situated (literally) at the seat of value-neutral social science, Lynd began to develop and sharpen his critique of empiricist social science from within, constantly urging his SSRC colleagues to be more socially relevant in their choice of issues and more willing to buck the cautionary, conformist pressures of major funders in spelling out the broader implications of their research.[29] Invited to contribute the chapter on consumer behavior for *Recent Social Trends*, Lynd found himself in the by-then familiar battle when, going beyond the blandly descriptive protocol followed in other chapters, he portrayed the largely unorganized, uneducated American consumer as beholden to business and advertising and called for a government agency to represent consumer interests.[30] Soon after the volume was completed and Herbert Hoover lost the presidency to Franklin D. Roosevelt, Lynd turned his expertise more directly into activism, as one of the experts, along with RSF's Leon Henderson, on the New Deal Consumer Advisory Board and its successor agency in the Department of Labor. Later, he helped in founding the Consumers' National Federation, an umbrella group of the consolidating consumer movement.[31]

Robert Lynd thus tapped a deep well of experience and, no doubt, frustration as something of a renegade in social science, when in 1938 he delivered the prestigious Princeton University Stafford lectures that would be the basis of *Knowledge for What*? At that point, however, he was preoccupied by the more dramatic portent of the worldwide arena, and his tone was one of deepening crisis and alarm. From beginning to end, the book is haunted by the specter raised in the very first paragraph and invoked until the very last: social science manipulated, abused, stripped of its intellectual freedom and ultimately conscripted into service by undemocratic political forces, as it had been by European fascism. This was a real and present danger in the United States, he warned, should the social sciences fail in their responsibility to provide the bold and vigorous intelligence needed to prevent the collapse of democratic values and institutions amidst panic over economic collapse. For that, they would need to get beyond the confines of narrow empiricism and abstract theory, beyond the confines of "practical politics" to ask "long-range and, if need be, abruptly irreverent questions of our democratic institutions."[32]

That American social science was failing to meet this responsibility was painfully clear to Lynd, and nowhere more than in the great contrast between the knowledge social scientists were producing and what society needed to know. Economists' failure to foresee the Great Depression was an infamous case in point. To Lynd, however, so was their refusal—or inability—to frame it as a broader crisis of capitalism so that Americans might look to more far-reaching or, in Lynd's mind, more centrally planned alternatives to see their way out. Lynd made a special target of economics, as the most scientistic and well-funded of the social sciences, but his critique had a broader sweep. The pursuit of a neutral and politically detached ideal of science, he thought, had made social science narrowly empirical, enamored of statistical technique, socially irrelevant in its abstracted theoretical apparatus—unwilling, above all, to ask questions that looked beyond the narrow confines of "what is" to imagine what might be. If anything, that timidity made social scientists less scientific, in Lynd's mind, in that it kept them from posing the kinds of hypotheses through which true scientific inquiry explored the otherwise unknown or unimagined. More important, it led social science to accept, rather than to challenge, prevailing definitions of the problem, and to be satisfied with "letting the facts speak for themselves." The effect, hardly politically neutral, was to leave the range of alternatives in the hands of those most vested in preserving the status quo.

Here, then, was the starting point for a more relevant, a more responsive, and, in Lynd's view, more approximately scientific social science. One component was more willingness to acknowledge the futility of achieving the objective certainty of the natural sciences. A second was more candor about how values and unexamined assumptions (as well as funding sources) shaped its research. The third, especially important, was more openness about what Lynd argued was the very purpose of social science—indeed, its very claim to legitimacy in a democracy—its uniquely "interested desire to know in order to do something about problems."[33] None of this was meant to suggest that social science should align itself with partisan politics or established interests, or even with a particular program of reform. Nor did it mean relinquishing the scientific tools of theorizing and empirical analysis. What it did mean was using those tools in a new way: to scrutinize and evaluate society's most cherished values, institutions, and reigning myths against the changing needs of democracy. For this, what society needed from social science, Lynd argued, was the knowledge to help "rewrite our institutions," including a "workable theory of cultural change" and the empirical research to understand what needed to change to "make real the claims of freedom and opportunity in America."[34]

To this end, Lynd concluded with a series of problems and "outrageous hypotheses" meant to illustrate how detached, dispassionate, and, in his view, ruthlessly honest empirical research could, when attached to the right questions and hypotheses, be a guide to democratic change. Here, in Lynd's unique, deliberately provocative, and fearless version of reframing the social question, was the link to the purposive tradition of reform investigation. Drawing his problems and hypotheses from life and social need rather than from academic discourse, Lynd mapped out an agenda for exploring, among other things, what organized yet democratic planning would look like and the dangers of muddling through; how democratic participation could be introduced to the increasingly large-scale bureaucracies of government, industry, and civic life; how to reform private capitalism for efficiency and the "general welfare"— and to escape the looming threat of fascism; how to discover and inculcate a sense of common purpose in a society of diminishing religious belief; and how to build a culture that recognizes its essential interdependence and the futility of war. Lynd looked to social scientific knowledge, that is, to know and to plan for the cultural, institutional, and political economic underpinnings of modern democracy.

It is hard to tell, though the deliberately caustic tone of *Knowledge for What?* offered a clue, just how serious Lynd was about translating his critique and "outrageous hypotheses" into a program for social scientific research and reform. Lynd himself did not pursue any major new empirical research projects and became increasingly alienated from academic culture. Still, for an idea of what it might have looked like we can go back to *Middletown,* which achieved what arguably no other work of social science, save possibly Henry George's *Progress and Poverty*, had to date. More than reflect, the book actually became part of the popular culture, subject of widespread popular discussion and even— though likely to Lynd's dismay—a major boon to the advertising industry. It also had impact, as the historian Sarah Igo argues, on the way people thought about themselves, as part of a cultural middle, or average, or mainstream—"Mr. and Mrs. John Citizen of Middletown, U.S.A."[35] Such discussion and language affected the way people thought about themselves, in ways that would continually be revisited. As social science, *Middletown* may not have accomplished the cultural work of New Deal reform, though that was clearly the objective by the time Lynd published *Middletown in Transition*. It did, however, go some ways toward popularizing the idea of a sociological or anthropological imagination, and trying, if not always succeeding, to use it as a new way of asking the old social question about the disparities between economic reality and democratic ideal.

Gunnar Myrdal: Facts and Valuations

The Swedish economist Gunnar Myrdal had already published his critique of value-neutral social science when the Carnegie Corporation invited him to come to the United States to head a major study of the American Negro in 1937.[36] In the lectures published in 1930 under the title *Vetenskap oc politik I nationalekonomien,* and two decades later in English as *The Political Element in the Development of Economic Theory,* he had boldly defied prevailing academic convention to reveal the value premises buried in neoclassical economics and to argue that social scientists should make explicit the otherwise hidden premises and valuations in their research. [37] This would begin a lifelong concern for Myrdal, one he would continually revisit and expand on in later work. The influence of values, he would argue, was not confined to the choice of question and the interpretation of data: values pervaded every aspect of research, from method, to analysis, to the very construction of "the social facts." Unlike Lynd, who in *Knowledge for What?* focused principally on the dangers and narrowness of value-neutral empiricism, Myrdal honed in on the fallacy of its premise. "There can never be, and has never been, a 'disinterested' research in the social field," he later wrote. "Valuations are, in fact, determining our work even if we manage to be unaware of it."[38]

Myrdal's concern about values in research was the framing principle of *An American Dilemma.* It was also, as American readers of the popular *Saturday Review of Literature* would learn from Robert S. Lynd, what made *An American Dilemma* the most influential work of social science on race relations or any other topic of the post–World War II era. In his review, Lynd called it "the most penetrating and important book on our contemporary civilization that has been written," a book "no one at all concerned with American democracy can afford to miss reading and pondering," adding, in what, given his own history with foundations, can be read only as a kind of backhanded dig, "close to the top among wise investments ever made by an American foundation."[39] To see why, he pointed readers to Myrdal's insistently moral approach.

What "objective" American economist of standing would ever have had the courage and insight to approach the Negro problem so? An appendix at the end of Volume II develops forcefully the general problem of the importance of values as a methodological instrument in social science. This appendix is good medicine for American social science huddling away from all value hypotheses and judgments lest its precious "objectivity" become polluted by life; and it should be made required reading in all university social science departments.[40]

That Lynd was so praiseful should come as no surprise. It is hard to imagine a more complete or fully realized expression of the purposive social science he envisioned. Certainly there was no rival—in scale, scope, ambition, and especially in visibility—at the time. *An American Dilemma* was densely, deeply empirical, pragmatic, theoretical and methodologically innovative, even interdisciplinary all at once. It had the deep pockets of an otherwise staid and cautious foundation to back it up—however insistently, and against all evidence to the contrary, Carnegie Corporation President Frederick P. Keppel claimed in the book's foreword that this was a case of letting the facts "speak for themselves."[41] Most important, it was an almost heroically self-conscious blend of value, scientific method, and fact. Myrdal made this clear from the beginning of the nearly 1,500-page tome, taking every opportunity to reiterate that this was to be far more than the survey of social conditions Carnegie may have expected at the start. Instead, it would be a basic restatement of the Negro problem as a fundamentally moral conflict in the collective conscience of white Americans. It would use its comprehensive survey of the status of American Negroes as a way to reflect on the whole of "American civilization" and hence make that the target of reform. It would develop a method for "a scientific approach which keeps the valuations explicit" and draws "practical conclusions" from valuations as well as facts.[42] It would also be explicit about the origins of its value premises, not in personal belief, but in the broader culture, as what Myrdal famously called the American Creed. This was Myrdal's way of making *An American Dilemma* relevant, of linking the so-called Negro problem in the United States to the social question writ large—the world-wide crisis of democracy and racist ideology being fought on the battlefields of World War II. It was also his way, as he noted in his introduction, of "enabling scientific study to arrive at true knowledge."

For Myrdal, then, values-conscious analysis was not unscientific or anti-empirical, or simply a way of acknowledging that valuations inevitably informed research. As he made plain in the methodological appendices Lynd referred to, making values explicit was actually both a deliberative scientific strategy and a necessity for accurate scientific research. To do otherwise, he noted with a quote from John Dewey, would be to obscure "the fundamentally moral nature of the social problem."[43] Still less was a values-based analysis about subordinating the analysis of data to preconceived premises. Myrdal had developed the moral dilemma framework relatively late in the project, and only after the empirical research was complete.[44] Indeed, the whole point of making valuations explicit was to keep them from "going underground" in the form of unexamined assumptions or biases stated as fact: in effect, to open them up for scrutiny and debate. Thus, Myrdal told his readers, the text of *An American Dilemma* would move continually between analyzing data and discussing the value premises underlying the analytic frame—highlighting the latter in italics to underscore their import. In the case of economic data, for example, that meant using empirical research to explore "the principal chasm between American ideals and practices: *that Negroes shall be awarded equal opportunities*" [emphasis in original]. Nor was this license for social scientists simply to impose their personal values on research. Myrdal acknowledged as much in his choice of the more typically American opportunity over a more social democratic notion of economic equality as his value frame. As he wrote with reference to his choice of the American Creed as a moral framework, *"The value premises should be selected by the criterion of relevance and significance to the culture under study"* [emphasis in original].[45] The value premises of social scientific research, though not dictated by the status quo, would themselves be held to a certain empirical as well as moral burden of proof.

It is by these criteria that Myrdal's reframing of the Negro problem comprises both the strengths and the limitations of his analysis. On the one hand, he offered a powerful argument for a more explicit recognition of values—democratic and not—that, when left unstated, did more to distort than illuminate the social facts. Those valuations in turn provided a powerful interpretive framework for making sense of an extraordinarily comprehensive range of empirical research on racial beliefs, on political and legal institutions, and on patterns of inequality and segregation. Myrdal also did not shy away from the overriding reason for making value premises explicit. No other subject was as "permeated by value judgments," Myrdal concluded in his extended "note" on social science and the Negro problem. No other subject had drawn such an elaborate array of rationalizations for complacency in the guise of value-free research. Indeed, to Myrdal, the most deep-seated bias in American social science was not scientific racism but the hidden bias toward "do-nothing (laissez-faire)" attitudes buried in Robert Park's and William Ogburn's naturalistic theories of change.[46] That those theories, which effectively undermined the case for purposeful action, had such enormous influence in the social sciences illustrated, to Myrdal, the power of the neutral social scientific framework simply to prevent the important debate from happening: the debate about race and democracy.

At the same time, considered as fact and as valuation, Myrdal's framework was flawed by its failure to grasp the deeply structural and institutional as well as cultural and psychological investment in white supremacy and by the overly optimistic belief in the power of its moral appeal. Myrdal would also subsequently come under criticism for treating African Americans, as well as the larger race problem, as themselves a "pathological" culture. In so doing, he opened the door to a wide array of similarly pathologizing research on the "damaged" black psyche that would take Myrdal as its justifying frame.[47] Equally troubling, especially to the largely unrecognized legions of movement activists who had been engaged in labor and civil rights organizing for generations, was Myrdal's failure to recognize black political agency. Within a framework in which blacks were pathological and whites had all the power, he

69

did not grasp the dynamics of the social movements that would galvanize the mobilization for racial democracy in the decades after *An American Dilemma* was first published. This failure was what prompted novelist Ralph Ellison to ask, in a memorable review, how it was possible for an entire "people. . . [to] live and develop for over three hundred years simply by *reacting*?"[48]

There was also, most uncomfortably, the fact that Myrdal might well have applied the value and analytic premises of the American Creed to the project he had just completed and to the knowledge establishment it represented. Indeed, one wonders whether Myrdal's extensive methodological notes, critical as they were of laissez-faire and "value-free" American social science, were a tacit recognition of the color line that put him—as a white European scholar with little knowledge of U.S. race relations and no record of research in the field, officially brought in as an outsider from a "neutral" country—in control of what would be the most massive and lavishly funded study of race relations conducted to date. Myrdal went out of his way to include African American scholars on the large research staff and to acknowledge their work. He also made it a point to be in contact with the major civil rights and civic organizations and their African American leadership. But Myrdal's value framework, at the time, proved more than the Carnegie Corporation was prepared to absorb. Using the same logic of disengagement and neutrality that Myrdal criticized, his philanthropic sponsor maintained a polite distance from the study and from its implications for white institutions and culture.[49]

It is somewhat ironic, then, that for all its flaws and for all that it left out, *An American Dilemma* would find its democratic, purposive potential as social science played out most fully in the hands of African American lawyers and activists who would use it to overturn the legal basis for Jim Crow. Myrdal's study would also find broad resonance within African American politics and civil society, where it would be used for movement-building as well as rhetorical purposes in the struggle to lay bare the consequences of the racial divide.

PART II

UNDERSTANDING THE CHALLENGE FROM THE RIGHT

To a degree that no doubt would have surprised them, the social scientists at the early Russell Sage Foundation and writing in the broader progressive tradition have a great deal to offer the project of social science and liberal philanthropy today. After all, though the progressives were not as unabashedly optimistic as they are sometimes made out to be, they were secure enough in their assumptions about social progress to imagine that a century later the need to study the labor question would have disappeared. Revisiting the dynamics the Pittsburgh surveyors and their contemporaries had called attention to in exploring the impact of sped-up production practices, the disappearance of job ladders, the gendered and racialized hierarchies in the workplace, the proliferation of home work and other informal modes of production, and, more generally, the gaps between low-wage earning and wealth owning America would also be unnecessary. Yet all of these issues have been subjects of recent RSF-funded research.[1] Nor would Gunnar Myrdal have expected that his morally resonant title would continue to be invoked, not merely as a point of reference but as a description of the contemporary race issue.[2]

Nothing would be more surprising to the foundation's founding generation, however, than to find its centenary counterparts grappling with the rise of an aggressively antistatist laissez-faire ideology, and with its unshakable hold on a now significantly reframed

71

social question. Ultimately, then, what gives Progressive-era social know-ledge its enduring—indeed, renewed—relevance is not continuity but change, embodied in the profound and ongoing transformations in political culture and public philosophy that have significantly altered the politics of knowledge and philanthropy over the past several decades and their ideological orientation. It is thus that I turn in the next three chapters to understand the historical roots of this transformation, and its expression in the rise of the philanthropic right.

✥ CHAPTER 3 ✥

Unsettling the Social Question: From Consensus to Counterrevolution in the Postwar Politics of Knowledge

Among the central conceits of the modern conservative movement has been to cast itself in counterrevolutionary terms. Nowhere does this play more loudly than from within the self-styled counterintelligentsia (vanguard of the counterrevolution) that for the last three decades has served the movement as a veritable fountainhead of conservative ideas and policy positions, a steady stream of editorial opinion, and—especially important—a keeper of the movement narrative and of its founding myths. As discussed more fully in chapter 5, the circuitry of activist intellectuals, think tanks, law institutes, journals, and foundations that anchors the conservative intelligentsia is itself the product of a self-consciously countermobilization launched in the 1970s. Of late, this now well-entrenched punditry has taken to writing its own history, if only to mark a slew of recently celebrated twenty-fifth year (the Heritage Foundation, the Cato Institute, the Manhattan Institute, for example) and other significant movement coming of age anniversaries (ten years of welfare reform). It is, by all accounts, a story of improbable triumph over the liberal Goliath, of tireless crusade against liberalism's most cherished conventional wisdoms, of irrevocably changing the policy conversation, of victory in the proverbial war of ideas. Told with the all the zestful hubris that the liberal knowledge establishment eschews, it is a story about changing history.[1]

Indeed, though its political influence is easily exaggerated, the ascendancy of the conservative knowledge and policy establishment is at this point beyond dispute. On issues ranging from social welfare to taxes to foreign policy and so-called family values, it has transformed and dominated the terms of policy debate. It has done so based on what is now a well-rehearsed script. First comes reframing issues as crises—of morality, of cultural degeneracy, and if at all possible of violated property rights. This is followed by vaulting a series of not long ago impossibly radical proposals— end welfare, privatize social security, eliminate the estate tax— from the fringes to the mainstream of policy alternatives. Its broader success, however, can also be measured in a historic role reversal that has transformed modern conservatism from an ideology of reaction to an ideology of radical reform, based on a program that envisions (and already is) rewriting the social contract to insist on individual self-reliance, private ownership, and a kind of sink or swim market morality as the guiding principles of public policy. All the while, policy intellectuals on the liberal-left spectrum confine themselves to a much-constricted sense of what politics and policy can possibly achieve. In doing so, they in effect make contemporary liberalism the ideology of (barely) staying the counterrevolution and maintaining what's left of the New Deal.

This transformation in political culture is hardly attributable to the conservative intelligentsia alone. It was, as the following chapters show, part of a broader political mobilization that brought organized constituencies together into an internally conflicted, but resilient political coalition. Nevertheless, the role of conservative intellectuals and the foundations that support them has been both pivotal and consistent over time. In the words of an aptly titled book by a movement admirer, to "think the unthinkable" in policy, and to use the apparatus of knowledge and policy making to bring the unthinkable about.[2]

I do not propose here to abandon the idea that the modern right should be seen as a counterrevolutionary movement. Indeed, the idea has staying power at least in part because it has considerable basis in reality. Among other things, it underscores the degree to which the modern conservative movement has deliberately defined itself in oppositional terms. Initially these came in response to Franklin D. Roosevelt's New Deal, the rise of Keynesianism, and the "collectivist" post–World War II welfare state, and subsequently in opposition to a series of "revolutions" in political economy and culture that conservatives fashion as threats to traditional American values. The list of threats and grievances has only grown and escalated in intensity over time. Today, it incorporates as well Lyndon B. Johnson's Great Society, the all-encompassing rights revolution—feminism, racial egalitarianism, the sexual revolution—and, of course, the moral laxity of the baby boom generation. Such threats have also been periodically (and conveniently) dramatized by association with or accusations of being soft on even more radically subversive enemies—communism, totalitarianism, terrorism—coming from outside what have only recently come to be called our homeland borders. But the more present and constant danger has remained the ideology of New Deal and postwar liberalism, conflated with the permissive counterculture and 1960s radicalism that liberalism presumably unleashed. At the heart of this ideological target, as we'll see, has been the philanthropic-government-academic establishment. This, in the political imagination of the modern right, is what provided liberalism with its institutional anchoring, its basic cultural orientation, and its most subversive ideas.

Yet even while adopting the "counter revolution" framework, I do call into question the way it has been deployed—in this case, as in the right's approach to knowledge more generally, for movement-building purposes. Certainly the call to counterrevolution provides the movement with a sense of mission as well as a unifying identity. It also stokes the fires of indignation and activism each time the call is repeated, in no small part by exaggerating the radicalism of the opposition and the immanence of its threat. In these ways, and equally important, the ongoing call to counterrevolution helps to hold together what are otherwise highly disparate elements within modern conservatism, joining moral traditionalists and free marketers in battle against a common enemy—liberalism—and in favor of a common cause: restoring the country to what conservative intellectuals have variously fashioned as its fundamentals, its core values, or its original intent. Indeed, in framing New Deal revolutions in political economy and law as subversions of traditional values and culture, the narrative of counterrevolution endows the conservative war of ideas with the spirit of a cultural if not a moral crusade. This in turn helps explain why the revolution in liberal policy, jurisprudence, and political economy can inspire as much oppositional fervor as the host of behavioral, cultural, and—especially—sexual revolutions the right attributes to the 1960s. In the oppositional consciousness of the conservative movement, they all stem from the same permissive, culturally relativist, liberal mindset. Particularly significant to understanding the role of knowledge in the movement, in linking all these revolutions to an all-powerful liberal elite, conservative intellectuals have been able and quite willing to tap into the movement's most parochial and anti-intellectual sentiments—even as they have worked to orchestrate an elite, intellectual mobilization in response.[3]

Thus, taken uncritically as a movement narrative, as one of modern conservatism's founding myths, the idea of conservative counterrevolution distorts as much as it reveals. Certainly, as noted, it greatly exaggerates the radicalism of the opposition. For all the changes they introduced, New Deal and Great Society liberalism were not even remotely revolutionary as ideological or political programs. They were far more attentive to the prerogatives of capital, white privilege, and fighting communism than conservatives would have us believe. More recently, and somewhat paradoxically, the same narrative that aims to dramatize liberalism's radicalism and all-pervasive power has been used to pronounce it a resounding failure as policy and as "big government" ideology—in this instance notably turning its attention away from more popular New Deal programs to the most controversial and politically vulnerable antipoverty and affirmative action programs of the Great Society. Here again, the narrative distorts and exaggerates in strategic ways. Despite its many limitations and failings, the Great Society launched a number of programs and legislative changes— Medicare, Medicaid, Head Start, the major civil rights acts, to name a few—that today continue to command majority support and anchor what is left of the federal commitment to economic security and racial justice. Nor can the Great Society, expansive as it was, be said to have been the radical program it has become in conservative demonology, except to the degree one considers the long overdue passage of legislation guaranteeing basic constitutional rights to racial minorities and women a radical departure from the past. After all, the leading weapon in the war on poverty was full employment and a tax-cut induced spurt of economic growth. Community action, a modestly funded initiative at best, was about giving poor people a voice in and access to the basic legal representation and social welfare services to which they, like other Americans, were entitled, at least at the time. What did give community action its radical potential—the loosely conceived notions of community empowerment, and maximum feasible participation—have subsequently been appropriated by champions of privatization and self-help. Notably, among the litany of liberal and Great Society failures, the conservative narrative does not include what the vast majority of historians would agree was LBJ's greatest policy failure, the war in Vietnam.[4]

Demonizing liberalism, however, is only one of the movement purposes served by counterrevolutionary tropes. It also hides what is truly radical, and political, about the conservative movement and its agenda. Indeed, the narrative of counterrevolution takes great pride in presenting the political rise of modern conservatism as a straightforward triumph of ideology and ideas, ironically aggrandizing the role of intellect at the expense of the properties—such as incentives, self-interest, and the profit motive—that in conservative political philosophy make capitalism and markets a force for the social good. Not surprisingly, it also inflates the importance of the people who are writing the narrative—the neoconservatives, the think tank punditry—in the movement and in history. It also obscures the degree to which the success of the counterrevolution in ideas had less to do with those individuals' inherent power or with conservatism's compelling vision and more with a combination of old-fashioned political coalition-building, a willingness to use knowledge to garner power in partisan politics and on behalf of elite business interests, and the ability of the first two to attract funding from a newly energized and newly organized philanthropic right.

The narrative obscures one other especially significant matter—the degree to which the right-wing knowledge and policy establishment has met with little effective resistance from its presumably still dominant, all powerful liberal counterpart. Instead, at each stage of the long process of organizing the postwar movement, the right has essentially, if inadvertently, been accommodated by liberalism's failure to understand, to acknowledge, or to take it seriously as much more than a bundle of impulses and resentments, let alone as a movement that might someday achieve the degree of political and cultural dominance it currently has.

It is therefore on a note of revision that I turn in these next chapters to consider the conservative counterrevolution in knowledge and philanthropy, the challenge it poses to the broadly liberal empirical knowledge tradition that Russell Sage and other foundations stand for, and why it warrants a more considered response. The rise of the right-wing research and policy establishment, I argue, needs to be recognized as more than simply a reactive, and not at all as a genuinely restorationist force. The political, economic, and moral order it invokes as tradition exists far more vividly in the conservative imagination than in historical reality. The conservative "counter" establishment also needs to be understood as part of a more radical ideological and political project, with a radical and activist agenda of its own. This is an agenda that is radical not simply in its aim to repeal the Great Society, the New Deal, liberal jurisprudence, progressive taxation, and even the modicum of corporate regulation introduced in the late nineteenth century—as William Greider recently put it, "to roll back the twentieth century" in social and economic policy.[5] It is radical in its goal to rebuild social and economic policy altogether, on an ideological base of individualism, free markets, and the sanctity of property rights, combined with state-sanctioned interventions to promote traditional, principally Christian, moral values. I also suggest a different way of understanding what has often been seen as a tension between the cultural and the political economic aims of the movement. From the start, I argue, the conservative counterrevolutionaries saw theirs as a fundamentally cultural project: not only in the traditional way we think of the culture wars as a battle over social values but also in attacking social science as a way of knowing, as a way of defining the public interest, and as a way of essentializing the values underlying the liberal consensus.

Social Science, the Liberal Consensus, and the "Problem" of Ideology

We need not look too far to understand why liberal social science has had trouble responding to the rise of the conservative policy-knowledge establishment, and to the ideological mobilization behind it. That is because one of the central projects, perhaps the defining project, of postwar social science was to marginalize if not literally define ideology out of existence as a legitimate force in American politics and culture. That project—apotheosized in the so-called end of ideology—was but one of the ways social scientists took part in constructing, and, whether intentionally or not, valorizing the idea of a broadly encompassing, marginally contested, pragmatic, and basically liberal ideological consensus in the roughly two decades after World War II. The other was to use the theoretical, methodological, and technical tools at hand to give liberalism and its core ideas the aura of an applied social science and an objective, nonideological body of knowledge. Thus neutralized by the alchemy of social science, the liberal consensus became the program of the growing philanthropic establishment and the constitutive center, as it were, of the postwar construction of neutrality in social scientific research. It also provided the prevailing framework for explaining—or, really, explaining away—the ideological right as an expression of a recalcitrant mood, an irrational politics of resentment or frustration or paranoia, as simply irrelevant, and in all cases not to be taken seriously.

As coined by the sociologist Daniel Bell in the late 1950s, the end of ideology was not at all the triumphalist statement later associated with such deliberately invocative post–cold war pronouncements as Francis Fukuyama's "the end of history."[6] Bell's subtitle, after all, announced that this was about the "exhaustion of political ideas," and the regrettable, if in his mind necessary, retreat from utopian visions of social democracy and the rule of reason as the postwar generation confronted the evils of holocaust, the power of the irrational as seen in rise of totalitarianism and in the power of nationalism as a politically unifying force. So, too, in Louis Hartz's equally iconic and influential *The Liberal Tradition* (1955)—which, like a number of other books at the time, pushed the idea of an essentially unopposed liberal consensus back to the founding of the American republic—one can read a lament for the absence of a politically viable left in the United States. Still, these and a number of other widely read (and often misread) books captured and lent an air of scientific authority to several intersecting assumptions underlying the dominant post–World War II political order. Such assumptions would in turn have important and lasting implications for the social scientific response to early glimmers of organized political and intellectual mobilization on the ideological right.

Most prominent among these was the conviction that, with the rise and extraordinarily destructive power of nazism and Soviet communism, ideologically driven movements of all sorts had revealed themselves to be highly dangerous—and all too often corrupt and illegitimate—as bases of political regimes. Postideological politics, in light of this revelation, would be based on the pluralistic give and take of discernable group interests and identities reflected in social scientific theories of political pluralism rather than on an animating set of big ideas. Postideological policy, by the same logic, would more than ever be shaped by nonaligned, nonideological expertise.

Accompanying this aversion to ideology was what in more popularized form was the more celebratory and optimistic assumption that, in the industrialized West if not in the rest of the world, the major ideological struggles had been settled once and for all, in favor of a widely shared commitment to political democracy, varying degrees of state-regulated capitalism, racial and ethnic pluralism, incremental improvement in the civil and political rights of women (if not full-blown gender equity), and a mildly redistributive welfare state. All were made possible, in the consensus view, by mass

prosperity and steady economic growth. Also settled, by implica-
tion, was the basic cultural commitment to the Enlightenment principles of rationality and scientific knowledge and to their authority
as guideposts to policy and social progress.

In another defining assumption, Bell and like-minded intellectuals advanced the idea that such pluralistic, ultimately consensual
politics were based not on any particular set of ideological commitments but on those universal human values and inclinations that,
as the engines of enlightenment, progress, and modernization,
could be used to overcome remnants of cultural backwardness or
ideological fundamentalism that stubbornly resisted the promise of
modernity as embodied in the industrialized West. Knowledge,
along with rationally conceived group interests, had come to replace ideology as a driving force in politics and culture. Similarly,
in postindustrial capitalism, it was coming to be celebrated as an
engine of economic growth. Engagement in making or acquiring
knowledge, indeed, was a signature feature of what liberal intellectuals from University of California President Clark Kerr to the
economist John Kenneth Galbraith were heralding as the rise of a
sort of postindustrial, even postcapitalist New Class. Kerr considered it an expression of the many practical and social uses to which
the expanding university could be put. Galbraith considered it evidence of the growing importance of work that produced personal
pleasure, intellectual growth, and cultural enrichment—qualitative, rather than quantitative goods—in a society that he hoped
would turn away from its obsession with mass production and con-
sumption to enjoy a better quality of life.[7] Later on, and ironically,
the concept and the politics of the New Class would figure promi-
nently in conservative efforts to unseat the liberal establishment.

Also underlying the end of ideology framework was the assumption that formal politics, nation states, and political economy constituted the terrain on which conflict and compromise might take
place, with culture, eros, and religion—currently lumped together
in the awkward category moral values—playing a subordinate role.
Indeed, this assumption was itself based on the idea that the boundaries between public and private had been essentially settled, and
that the private by definition was somehow immune to the kind of

ideological contestation and mobilization that would gain traction in the essentially rational, interest-driven political realm.

A final assumption, and indeed the one that made all the others seem possible, was the idea that the same advances in technology and knowledge that heralded the emergence of a restructured, widely described as advanced, postindustrial economy had brought the achievement of permanent and widely shared prosperity within reach. Although not nearly as uncritically celebrated as the appellation suggests, the sheer fact of material abundance highlighted in John Kenneth Galbraith's "affluent society" seemed to hold out a tantalizing prospect. The old, perplexing social questions of poverty, of labor, even, for some, of race might be peacefully resolved within the framework of democratically managed capitalism—the "people's capitalism," as trumpeted by Vice President Richard Nixon in debate with Soviet Premier Nikita Khrushchev, and in such bastions of corporate America as the Advertising Council and *Fortune* magazine—if not relegated to the past.[8]

If these assumptions made it difficult to anticipate and take seriously the currents that would animate the resurgent right, it is at least in part because they also put social science so thoroughly at the vital center of the postwar liberal project. That position was one a number of social scientists occupied with growing confidence. What they had to offer the postwar liberal polity by way of practical theory and objective, neutral expertise, and—with growing assurance from the reconstituted Russell Sage Foundation, among others—rigorous, theorctically rooted knowledge as opposed to its merely applied social scientific counterpart was more important than ever in meeting society's increasingly complex needs.

Of these needs, none was more important than the need to recalibrate—fine-tune, if you will—the boundaries of the older, more associationalist version of the new liberalism to accommodate the increasingly state-centered social welfare, labor, infrastructure-building, regulatory, and planning commitments fought over and forged in response to the crises of Great Depression and World War II and at the heart of FDR's New Deal. The product of crisis and political compromise more than any overarching or internally coherent scheme, those commitments nevertheless involved some major shifts in ideology and public philosophy. This was especially so with regard to the role and responsibilities of the federal government in the economy and in the lives of citizens. But neither were they at all revolutionary. Envisioned most expansively in FDR's Economic Bill of Rights—to a job, decent housing, health care, economic security, a living wage—as well as in a cluster of wartime economic and resource planning agencies, those commitments would come to settle on the more restrained, corporatist principles of growth-oriented economic management, full (or close to full) employment, and a decidedly public-private, compensatory, but still more federally centralized welfare state. To this would eventually be added, albeit on a far more tentative, deeply contested basis, and with no meaningful legislative apparatus until the 1960s, a largely rhetorical commitment to Myrdalian racial assimilationism.

Second, and ever a source of tension with economic and racially liberal commitments, was the need to contain the Soviet threat, and especially to keep it from spreading to the developing world. This, too, would engage social science in an ongoing project of ideological recalibration, as cold war liberalism turned more aggressively to reaffirm its allegiance to capitalism and to equate it with political democracy and freedom. But the cold war also generated massive demands for social scientific knowledge from within the expanding national security state, and in the globalized battle for military superiority as well as for hearts and minds.[9]

Finally, there was the need to confront the enduring dilemmas of economic, political, and especially racial democracy. All had been made more stark by the direct confrontation with racist regimes in World War II and by the fear of giving the Soviets a weapon in cold war propaganda battles. Equally important, though, and equally stark in the context of cold war, was to contain the movements these deep and enduring inequalities might inspire—not only by responding to root causes but by convincing those left out of the postwar promise of affluence and opportunity that they could realize their objectives within the framework of liberal pluralistic politics, a policy program focused on economic growth, a gradually more inclusive welfare state, and a nonsocialist, liberal ideological consensus.

To these various and changing needs, postwar philanthropy responded by redoubling its commitment to the social and behavioral sciences, in the faith that better knowledge about individual and group behavior and cultures would provide answers to the thorniest problems of global conflict and domestic unrest, even while helping spread democracy and capitalist economic development. Especially in the context of the expanding welfare state, better knowledge, rather than direct social betterment, would be postwar philanthropy's special provenance.

Moreover, postwar philanthropy in general, and social science foundations, RSF in particular, were operating in a much-altered political economy of research. Despite lingering suspicions among politicians, federal dollars poured into the behavioral and social sciences as never before, much of it from the military agencies, and much of it related to cold war concerns. The social sciences became institutionalized within the expanding federal government as well, in institutions such as the National Institute of Mental Health, in research offices within just about every major federal agency, and even, after some struggle, within the National Science Foundation. Although all of the major disciplines were affected by the new federal largesse, economics remained the standard-bearer for the policy sciences, and at the newly established (1946) president's Council of Economic Advisers, the most powerful expression of the discipline's newfound prestige in Washington.[10]

If this influx of government funding left the major old-line foundations feeling dwarfed, they also had to contend with the postwar arrival of the behemoth Ford Foundation, which had grown from a Michigan-based family operation to by far the country's largest private philanthropy in the late 1940s. In 1949, Ford announced its intention to devote an unspecified portion of its $500 million in assets to "improved scientific knowledge of individual human behavior and human relations."[11] The older foundations, for their part, began to think more in terms of "leveraging" other public and private dollars and using their own resources more "strategically."[12] Thus would RSF, here coordinating with other major foundations, position itself to expand the nongovernmental infrastructure of the behavioral sciences through institutions such as the Center for Advanced Studies in the Behavioral Sciences in Palo Alto. Equally significant, it would work to institutionalize the social sciences and social scientific thinking within civil society and professional practice. The foundations, with RSF very much at the helm, also began to think of themselves as part of a distinctive sector that could be studied and coordinated and (preferably self-) regulated in its own right. "Watching" philanthropy became one of the emphases of RSF's reconstituted postwar program.[13]

Social science, in turn, responded by redoubling its commitment to becoming a true science of society and here more than ever aspiring to the status of the natural and physical sciences. This would involve social science, in the Russell Sage Foundation's aptly militaristic phrase, in the "second trench" rather than on the front lines of social problem solving. Building up the infrastructure of social science, in its new postwar thinking, would simply be another way of fulfilling the commitment to "the improvement of social and living conditions in the United States of America" envisioned in the original charter. Funding for social welfare would shift to providing the underlying analysis but refraining from direct engagement in reform.[14] Without abandoning the commitment to empirical research, this would mean redoubling the emphasis on theory and method. Not, to be sure, in the grand tradition of Marx so much as in the pragmatic tradition of what the sociologist Robert Merton called theories of the middle range: focused, empirically verifiable, applicable to real world situations and problems, and generally applicable within the parameters of existing institutions and political arrangements. Thus would postwar social science not so much retreat as reposition itself in the project of liberal reform while maintaining an official commitment to objective neutrality.

Of course, the major theories that formed the bedrock of the postwar behavioral and social sciences were hardly devoid of ideological or political commitment. Those commitments, however, were expressed as conceptual frameworks, as hypotheses, or as statements of empirical fact. Much as theories of pluralism became the basis of political analysis as well as affirmations of political values, so, too, were theories meant to explain modernization steeped in the values of progress, technology, and the stages of capitalist economic development they theorized.[15] Nor was it by coincidence that the most influential theories of the postwar era would find a way to reconcile, if not essentialize, the links between capitalism and political democracy, freedom and the centralized state, and individual and collective (public) interest. Social problems and inequality, in what the sociologist C. Wright Mills memorably called the "professional ideology of social pathologists" could be understood as aberrations from a system that otherwise functioned to promote opportunity.[16] In keeping with the value-free tradition, however, such connections and affirmations would be formulated as empirical research findings rather than as ideological or value statements.

Social scientists would also contribute to the postwar liberal project in two other ways that contributed to and reinforced its aura of applied knowledge and technocratic neutrality. One was through the vast expansion of the contract research industry, itself largely based in cold war demands for strategic, analytic knowledge, and heralded by the creation of the Rand Corporation, the contract research organization that truly put the terms *expert* and *think tank* on the map.[17] By the early 1960s, the Rand model was being exported to domestic policy and imported into government research offices in the form of systems analysis, the "revolutionary" new method said to have put defense policy on a strictly rational, cost-benefit basis and soon to be tapped by the Johnson administration to revolutionize domestic policy as well. Enthralled by the notion of turning policy making into an exact science, administration officials recruited systems analysts from the Rand Corporation to show them how to win the war on poverty. They established analytic research offices within key antipoverty agencies, and created "domestic Rand corporations"—the University of Wisconsin's Institute for Research on Poverty and the Urban Institute—as their outside counterparts. As *Business Week* quipped, these were the "think tanks that think for the poor." By the late 1960s, just before welfare reform was to become a thirty-year national obsession, they came up with a rational and cost-beneficial way of ending poverty by 1976, a negative income tax that would provide a guaranteed minimum income for all Americans.[18] It was not long before such technocratic optimism would meet its match in the fiercely ideological politics of poverty, race, and welfare reform, as I discuss in more detail in chapter 4. For now, I note simply that systems analysis was but one of the expanding array of similarly exportable, decontextualized research technologies that, much like globalizing theories such as modernization, offered a universalist vision of democratic governance and policy making, indeed of state-building, that could presumably transcend if not replace cultural norms, ideologies, and politics in U.S. efforts to form common cause with the third world.

The other way social science contributed to postwar liberalism's technocratic sensibility was in offering a way of engaging—and constructing—the democratic public that was itself increasingly technocratic and abstracted from context of everyday life. Mediated by ever more sophisticated, institutionalized, and national public opinion polling technologies, the idea of the representative or average American public was in reality based on highly selective samples that conformed to a vision of an affluent, consensus-bound society, and that systematically left out perspectives from low-income and nonwhite Americans. At the same time, the public role of social science was becoming less and less about engaging with, educating, and in the broadest Deweyan sense empowering an informed, democratic public. It was instead focusing more and more on speaking truth to power through institutionalized venues of expertise such as think tank or official advisory agencies.[19]

Of all that social science had to contribute to the postwar liberal project, however, none was more important or emblematic of a technocratic sensibility than Keynesian economics. It promised just the right combination of theory, analytic method, and confident expertise to provide a program of growth and prosperity with the help of fine-tuning fiscal policy tools. Yet, the much-vaunted Keynesian consensus was not simply adopted as a matter of course, or of science. It was a product of considerable debate, intellectual entrepreneurship, and internal politicking within the key agencies of economic policy advice.[20] The triumph of Keynes as the new New Economics in turn had an impact on how standards of objectivity and neutrality were set. The once anti–New Deal Brookings

Institution, for example, reorganized substantially to bring itself into the postwar ideological mainstream and by the 1960s had recruited an impressive group of Keynesian economists and government officials with liberal credentials, in the process strengthening ties to liberal philanthropy and to such powerful executive branch agencies as the Council of Economic Advisers.[21]

Thus, in envisioning themselves as neutral and objective truth-tellers in a much-changed postwar political environment, social scientists and their philanthropic patrons were working from a distinctive framework of ideas and ideological consensus. That framework was shaped by a combination of liberal Keynesianism, pluralism, anticommunism, and confidence that social science had the technical know-how to sustain shared prosperity, economic growth, and to avoid crippling recessions—as well as to bring the benefits of such know-how to the world. It was a framework within which certain ideas were just so thoroughly discredited as to be beyond contention. Even the editors of *Fortune* were prepared to treat those ideas as relics of a woebegone past. In *U.S.A., The Permanent Revolution* (1951), a book that itself has come to be seen as something of a cold war relic, the editors dismissed the idea that the United States would ever want to return to laissez-faire liberalism, the reign of the robber barons, the era of unmitigated class warfare, of Darwinian struggles for survival, and vast unmet needs. The "transformation of American capitalism" was permanent and consensual, characterized most fully by the idea that "ownership carries social obligations" beyond making a profit.[22] Other ideas, by the same token, had such a firm basis in scientific knowledge and political consensus as to be similarly beyond serious, legitimate intellectual dispute: the mixed if still decidedly capitalist economy, the compensatory and public-private welfare state, and the pluralistic and secularized common culture based on the values of rational enlightenment. In either case, knowledge was on the side of a seemingly nonideological liberalism, of pluralistic political consensus, of gradualistic knowledge-based reform. Challenges from outside the circumscribed ideological consensus could be ignored, or explained away as irrational, or, in the case of the social democratic left in particular, marginalized as unrealistic or potentially subversive.

For these reasons, among others, the logic of social scientific neutrality was not only misleading, but also highly limited in its capacity for understanding or dealing with social movements from outside the ideological center. On the one hand, it suppressed contending visions of democracy from within the liberal consensus. On the other, it left social scientists with a limited repertoire of explanations for what, in the title that has become the emblematic expression of the liberal consensus view, the editor Daniel Bell referred to as "the new American right." In a collection of essays first issued in 1955 and featuring contributions from such consensus school stalwarts as the historian Richard Hofstadter, the political scientist Seymour Martin Lipset, and Bell himself, the right was largely depicted in psychological terms and as an irrational force.[23] In Hofstadter's later, memorable phrase, what joined the Goldwater right to the McCarthy right and both to the populist right was a peculiarly "paranoid style" rooted in the psychology of resentment, anger, and antimodernism.[24]

Additional issues kept liberal social scientists from taking the right seriously as an ideological force. One was that to do so would violate their deepest cultural assumptions and commitments to the superiority of rational inquiry and debate especially. Another was that, especially after Senator Joseph R. McCarthy's self-destruction and through well after Barry Goldwater's resounding presidential defeat in 1964, it appeared there was no reason to. But it was also the case that responding to ideological challenges in any but the most neutrally scientific terms would involve social scientists and their philanthropic patrons in politically controversial disputes. And it would require that they admit to having ideological commitments in the first place.

Seeds of Counterrevolution

Shortsighted though it may appear in retrospect, explaining the right as a reactionary fringe element was something the right seemed to invite upon itself. Its most visible spokesmen, after all, specialized in the politics of hysteria and rhetorical extremism that led John Birch Society founder Robert Welch to include President

Dwight D. Eisenhower on his list of communist conspirators, Senator Strom Thurmond to head a third-party presidential campaign on a white supremacist platform in 1948, and William F. Buckley to define a conservative as one who stood athwart history yelling "Stop!" in the inaugural issue of the journal that would play a defining role in the movement, the *National Review*. What's more, and only adding more fuel to the right-wing fire, a good deal of comparatively "respectable" or moderate conservatism could be accommodated within the loose liberal consensus. This included, for a time, a fair proportion of what could be considered the dominant, moderate wing of the Republican party, the corporate liberals who had made their peace, even if reluctantly, with the New Deal welfare state, the kind of soft segregationists who, as Gunnar Myrdal knew well, opposed discrimination in principle while practicing it in reality, and the white-shoe lawyers and business executives who served on foundation boards. Little wonder, then, that the initial response to right-wing attacks on liberalism and liberal social science was, when not marginalizing or ignoring them, to dismiss them as the rantings of a radical fringe—to position the neutral voice of reason and moderation against the conspiratorial anticommunists, the rabid segregationists, and the irrational reactionaries. Yet it is also in those initial encounters that we see the first, effectively stage-setting elements of what only later came together as the core themes of a more organized conservative opposition, from the moral critique of the culturally "relativist" pragmatism underlying empirical research to the resurgence of free market ideology. It is also in these early encounters that we see what would be the characteristically neutral liberal response.

The Revolt Against Pragmatism

Among the most visible right-wing volleys against liberal social science came in the course of a red-baiting campaign against the "big foundations"—as the prominent philanthropoid Waldemar Neilsen would later designate Rockefeller, Carnegie, Ford and some thirty others with assets of more than $100 million. Though always lightning rods for progressive and populist critique, during the postwar years foundations were growing rapidly in assets and ambition, making them increasingly visible on the national political scene.[25] In back-to-back congressional hearings launched in the early 1950s by Eugene Cox (D-GA) and B. Carroll Reece (R-TN), investigators promised the most extensive inquiry since Frank P. Walsh's 1915 Commission on Industrial Relations. The purpose was to learn whether foundations were acting as "enemies of the capitalistic system" by funneling their tax-exempt dollars to left-wing causes and scholars, or harboring more subversives like the recently convicted Alger Hiss—president of the Carnegie Endowment for Peace—in their midst.[26] Of course, such suspicions were a far cry from what had led Walsh's Progressive-era commission to accuse John D. Rockefeller of using his foundations to consolidate Standard Oil Company's power and wealth. But even more than the much-changed political environment of the cold war 1950s, the Cox and Reece charges underscored three motivating factors that would continue to be salient as motivation for right-wing attacks.

One was that the most prominent foundations—with good reason—had become emblems of the eastern establishment that, critics charged, drew an overwhelmingly WASP, male, Ivy League educated group of bankers, corporate executives, lawyers, government officials, and assorted privileged professionals and intellectuals together in a series of "interlocking directorates" through which they exerted enormous control over the nation's political, economic, and cultural life. As such, foundations like Carnegie, Rockefeller, and the recently created, comparatively gargantuan Ford Foundation stood as especially effective targets for galvanizing the combination of political and cultural conservatism and economic populism that fueled right-wing politics. Second, seen at the time as venues for linking the moderately centrist Eisenhower wing of the Republican party with New Deal liberals, foundations became battlegrounds in efforts to move Republicans to the right. Third, and equally important though only obliquely acknowledged at the time, in the wake of such visible, if painfully cautious and oblique foundation endorsements of racial integration as Gunnar Myrdal's *An American Dilemma*, charges of subversive activities in foundations became barely disguised measures to attack efforts to challenge the prevailing segregationist order. All three factors were at work in the 1954 Reece committee investigations. These widely publicized inquiries, following the largely exculpatory conclusions of the earlier Cox investigations, were principally aimed at the ultra-establishment Carnegie, Rockefeller, and Ford foundations. They were launched with the support of conservative, segregationist southern Democrats and hard-right Taft Republicans. Having found evidence of a "diabolical conspiracy" to "indoctrinate" Americans with collectivist views, they singled out the role of "socialist" Myrdal's *An American Dilemma* in the Brown v. Board of Education decision as evidence of overreaching "scientism" invading the Supreme Court.[27]

Actually, Myrdal's was but the most incendiary of the many prominent foundation-sponsored studies swept up in the committee's broadside indictment of the social scientific enterprise, an indictment that included *An American Soldier* (commissioned by the U.S. Army), Alfred Kinsey's best-selling and headline-grabbing "sex studies" (funded by the Rockefeller Foundation, which subsequently withdrew support), the Encyclopedia of the Social Sciences, and just about anything ever associated with the Social Science Research Council, the philosophy of John Dewey, and the term *behavioral science*. What made Myrdal and Kinsey and even *An American Soldier* obvious targets—race, sex, Freud, patriotism, and Swedish social democracy—is less interesting than the labels that brought them together. Indeed, what they (presumably) shared is an indicator of the political purposes such labels were meant to serve. Social science, the Reece committee reported as one of its official findings, was evidence of "the excess of empiricism" in foundations and within the wider knowledge industry. Underlying the "overindulgence" was the fallacy that social problems had social scientific solutions. More to the point was empiricism's corrosive influence on "basic and fundamental principles, religious, ethical, moral and legal." The issue was not so much, then, that the research was value free as that it provided scientific license to the wrong values—values subversive to free enterprise as well as to "our Judeo Christian moral system," and now, thanks to the influence of foundations and their interlocking research networks, the basis of liberal jurisprudence and social policy.[28]

The cascading connections between liberalism and godless social science would only harden and grow more conspiratorial in the ever-expanding but basically consistent litany of charges against foundations and social science that, levied to little avail in the McCarthyite hearings, were subsequently kept up in right-wing organizations and media outlets. The litany was laid out in any number of right-wing screeds. One was penned by Archibald Roosevelt, grandnephew of Theodore. The one perhaps most fully expounded, however, came from attorney and self-described "professional anti-Communist" Rene A. Wormser, who had served as special counsel to the Reece committee. In 1958, after those hearings dissolved amidst fierce and embarrassing committee infighting, Wormser published his own exposé. Echoing critics on the right, he referred to a revolution in policy and culture that the foundations had orchestrated. Under the guise of devoting philanthropic resources to the general welfare, he maintained, the nation's largest and most prominent foundations were funneling their vast reservoirs of tax-exempt money into a wider network of research and educational organizations that aimed to spread a credo of collectivist New Dealism, internationalist one-worldism, and dangerous, culturally relativist social scientific empiricism on an unsuspecting public. Deeply subversive of individual freedom and capitalist enterprise, they were using their unchecked economic power to reorient American culture and politics, in collusion with a host of universities, learned societies, policy research organizations, and that most subversive of organizations, the national Parent-Teachers Association. Most shocking of all, as *New York Daily News* columnist John O'Donnell put it in 1954, "was that the huge fortunes piled up by such giants as John D. Rockefeller, Andrew Carnegie, and Henry Ford were today being used to destroy or discredit the free-enterprise system which gave them birth."[29] At the helm of this silent revolution was a growing cadre of foundation professionals and social scientists—scions of what in other contexts would be called the New Class—who, while claiming to operate in the public interest, were in fact recasting it to fit their own collectivist worldview. The most that could be hoped for, Wormser concluded, was a counterrevolution, perhaps funded by the handful of foundations "unorthodox enough to support conservative writers and projects."[30]

As Wormser noted, there were such dedicated conservative foundations at the time, though, with the exception of the funds controlled by the likes of J. Howard Pew and Howard L. Hunt, they were comparatively small and deliberately disconnected from the reigning policy establishment. Nor did battle cries like Wormser's seem likely to succeed where Congressman Reece—"the David who had the courage to face the foundation Goliaths and their serried ranks of defenders"—had so resoundingly failed.[31] Wormser tempered his calls for counterrevolution with a plea to businessmen who served as foundation trustees to come to their senses and change things from within, a plea that would be echoed in later efforts to establish a countervailing philanthropic force.

Yet, for all that makes these particular McCarthy-era attacks on social science easy to dismiss (and in large part they were dismissed, especially in the witch-hunting weary mainstream press) two thing draw our attention about their significance for the counterrevolution to come. One is the bedrock of charges animating the attack. These—cultural relativism, liberal interlock, subversive values, and anti-Americanism—would, as reiterated and repackaged over the ensuing decades, continue to fuel conservative attacks on the liberal academy. Although at the time largely confined to right-wing publications and organizations, this compendium of conspiratorial charges would also unite conservative movement intellectuals around a sense of shared victimization—a feeling confirmed, to *National Review* editor Frank Meyer, by the explanations liberal social science offered for the conservative holdouts. Responding to the initial publication of Bell's *The New American Right*, Meyer argued that it was not the right but the liberal social scientists who suffered from a case of neurotic delusion. "[Because] all political, economic and social prepositions that form the accepted corpus of liberal thought are beyond intellectual doubt or question, the only explanation of dissent must be, in the liberal fantasy, a psychological defect, approaching, it is often hinted, paranoia."[32] The charges, replete with the sense of victimization, would resurface more visibly amidst the turmoil of war, racial violence, social protest, and counterculture of the late 1960s. They would resurface once again in academic culture wars of the 1980s, this time with a more respectable pedigree, and with conservative foundation support.

The other significant feature of the McCarthy-era attacks was the way the foundations responded to even the most hysterical charges against their programs, staff members, and grantees. The Carnegie Corporation's defense of *An American Dilemma*, for example, did not vigorously back Myrdal's argument or its underlying values but retreated behind his objectivity as a social scientist, his neutrality as an outsider studying American race relations, and the pro-Americanism of his invocation of the American Creed. The desire to maintain neutrality, in turn, would lead foundations to curb or distance themselves or to end funding for their more controversial grantees, in effect accommodating their ideological critics in the course of defending their own ideological neutrality.[33]

Launching the Battle of Ideas

However, in at least some venues, Wormser's counterrevolutionary aspirations did not seem so unanchored or premature. Far removed from the congressional spotlight, elements of a more serious, albeit still sporadically organized intellectual opposition were taking form. Financed for the most part by comparatively obscure funders, such scattered efforts were dedicated initially to preserving and—later, with gathering momentum—to spreading a handful of conservative ideas held together by their common animosity toward New Deal and postwar liberalism. These were the ideas about free market capitalism, individual liberty, limited government, and moral traditionalism that, though in some ways internally conflicted, would form the ideological core of the conservative counterrevolution, and on which the self-appointed counterintelligentsia of a later generation would draw again and again and again. Indeed, we can also see the kernel of an emerging battle plan that would bring conservatism's contradictory impulses together and later escalate into a full-scale war of ideas.

This conjoining of (some) of conservatism's contradictory impulses was among the central contributions of by far the most important of the scattered postwar conservative idea venues, the international gathering known as the Mont Pelerin Society (MPS). Until the wave of conservative institution-building in the 1970s, no other venue was as persistent or broadly influential in its support for the idea that unregulated market capitalism and market relations more generally were what made political freedom possible. Both required an active legal and cultural commitment to limited government as well as to the social institutions—albeit not a government-enforced one—that would allow market relations to flourish in public and private life.[34] That said institutions would include such conservative standard bearers as religion and the traditional family was not a constitutive element of free market thought. That they might be construed as such was a tantalizing possibility for conservative intellectuals, however. It was certainly one that later conservative activists, in particular the neoconservatives, would aggressively pursue.

The key early figure here was Friedrich August von Hayek, Austrian economist and product of the free market-oriented Austrian school of economics. Hayek was and is still internationally acclaimed by free market devotees as the author of the improbable best-selling book (thanks to the condensed version serialized in *The Reader's Digest*) *The Road to Serfdom* (1944).[35] This was what most firmly established Hayek as the hero of the anti-Keynesian, anti–New Deal right. In it, he not only made the case for what in prevailing economic thought was considered a thoroughly discredited philosophy of classical economic and political liberalism. He also denounced state-centered economic planning as market-defying collectivism and an authoritarian accumulation of power. Planning, as such, was the first irrevocable step on the road to individual servitude and political totalitarianism. Hayek also made a distinction, however, between the market liberalism he was advocating and libertarian antistatism or the traditional doctrine of laissez-faire. Like other influential free market economists at the time, including the University of Chicago's Henry Simons, Hayek argued that the modern version of classical economic liberalism (what today is known as neoliberalism) required a positive and active commitment on the part of the state to providing the legal, and in some cases even the social policy, framework for making market competition the central organizing principle for economic, social, and political life.[36] Such a "positive" case was necessarily tempered, however. Hayek was extremely skeptical about another key plank in the postwar liberal (and philanthropic) edifice, the concept of an overriding public interest beyond that in the freedom to make choices in competitive market conditions.

Hayek also burnished his reputation as free market hero with what would turn out to be his most successful act of intellectual entrepreneurship in a career otherwise conducted within the confines of the academy. In this, in addition to the luster he gained from *The Road to Serfdom*'s improbable success, a critical element was the stance he cultivated as a renegade among academic economists, an isolated voice for economic freedom in wartime London (where he had joined the faculty of the London School of Economics in 1931) and later, with his younger colleague Milton Friedman as a faculty member at the University of Chicago, in the postwar United States. In 1947, Hayek parlayed his growing reputation into the founding of the Mont Pelerin Society. Named for the site of what became its first annual meeting in Switzerland (the source of the original business financing) the MPS quickly became the leading international outpost for free market thinkers from the United States and Europe. It boasted regular attendance from academics, lawyers, former government officials, and—especially significant for the future course of the anti-Keynesian counterrevolution—from wealthy businessmen such as the British industrial chicken farm entrepreneur Antony Fisher, author of the Hayek-inspired anti-Keynesian book *The Case for Freedom* (1947). With Hayek's encouragement, Fisher would go on to establish what is now a global network of free market think tanks. One of these was London's Institute for Economic Affairs, established in 1955 and later credited, along with the Centre for Policy Studies, as Margaret Thatcher's brains trust. Another was the Manhattan Institute, established in New York in 1978 and the launch pad for both Charles Murray's *Losing Ground* and George Gilder's rhapsodic ode to supply-side economics

Wealth and Poverty, among many others.[37] Hayek himself would go on to join Milton Friedman, Frank Knight, and others to make the Chicago School of Economics the academic headquarters of classical economic liberalism in the United States—albeit from an extradepartmental appointment as professor of social and moral science in the interdisciplinary Committee on Social Thought and with extramural funding from the free market Volker Fund. The major impact on the conservative counterrevolution. however, would eventually come through the extra-academic channels Hayek helped inspire. Also important were the activist intellectuals who would use his *Road to Serfdom* as a touchstone for their efforts. They aimed to do exactly what he, like Milton Friedman, argued needed to be done to create the conditions for free market competition to prevail in the United States: to transform and use the institutions of political economy, law, policy, governance and, for some, of civil society to realize their vision of freedom. The many unresolved tensions in this project—its use of the state to protect the principle of limited government; its vision of the tradition-melting market as the basis of a well-ordered society—would be outweighed by the imperative of opposing liberalism.

Few were more aware of these tensions than the Harvard University economist Joseph Schumpeter, whose wartime work would also establish his place—albeit a somewhat more ambiguous one—in modern conservatism's intellectual pantheon, and provide inspiration for ideas later deployed in the counterrevolution. Schumpeter is perhaps best known for his aphoristic celebration of capitalism's "creative destruction," the constant innovation required for economic progress and growth. That idea, along with Schumpeter's emphasis on the importance of creative entrepreneurs, would provide inspiration in the exuberant market revivalism and supply-side economic logic of the Reagan era.[38] But another element of Schumpeterian irony would later emerge in the neoconservative critique of—and strategy for counteracting—the so-called New Class that liberals like Clark Kerr and John Kenneth Galbraith held forth as a force for social enlightenment. That was Schumpeter's argument that capitalism, by its very success, was sowing the seeds of its own destruction. On the one hand, it gave rise to the managerial rationalism that was paving the way to socialism. On the other, and more significant, it created the cultural conditions for the emergence of an anticapitalist intellectual elite—mostly academic, resentful and alienated from the business acumen of the entrepreneurial bourgeoisie, and dedicated to cultivating the anticapitalist ethos within the broader culture that would ultimately lead to capitalism's defeat. In perhaps the ultimate ironic twist, the neoconservative activist Irving Kristol and others would later use this idea to convince business conservatives that they needed to cultivate a new class of their own—in the interest, in effect, of unsowing the seeds of destruction Schumpeter foreshadowed.

Clearly important in the genesis of conservative movement ideas, the influence of figures such as Hayek and Schumpeter is also significant for what it tells us about the role of knowledge in modern conservatism's postwar oppositional culture, and about the use of knowledge in the emerging counterrevolution. Both of these Austrian émigrés had well-established reputations as empirical economists. It was as political philosophers, writing about particular ideas of capitalism in relation to individual freedom and democracy, however, that they saw themselves making their most significant mark—as, later on, would Milton Friedman in his consensus-defying tome *Capitalism and Freedom* (1962) and the more popularized and polemical *Free to Choose* (1980) coauthored with Rose Friedman.[39] As economists they were not in the same camp as the anti-empirical right. Friedman, after all, wrote extensively about monetary flows, and their history, in influential work that would eventually help shift the emphasis away from Keynesian fiscal policy instruments. Despite this, they had a distinctly nonempirical concept of their role as free market, and ultimately as erstwhile movement intellectuals. This was to defy and replace conventional wisdom and existing policy not with empirical research but with deliberately provocative big ideas. "Political philosophy," as the historian Jerry Muller puts it, "was the art of making the seemingly impossible politically plausible."[40]

This way of thinking about the role of knowledge in turn brings a certain significance to another idea rooted in conservatism's postwar oppositional moment that would later be resurrected in now-familiar counterrevolutionary phraseology. The phrase in question originated with the publication of *Ideas Have Consequences* (1948) by Richard Weaver (who reportedly didn't much like the title) the alienated and unapologetically unreconstructed southern traditionalist who also spent most of his academic career as an instructor of composition and rhetoric at the University of Chicago, and whose book would make him one of the most important figures in postwar conservative thought.[41]

Save for his abiding animosity toward New Deal liberalism and Deweyan pragmatism, Weaver had little intellectually or even ideologically in common with the free market right. Along with figures such as Russell Kirk and the émigré philosopher Leo Strauss, Weaver anchored the profoundly antimodern, so-called traditionalist right—the wing that looked to Edmund Burke, to the ancient philosophers, and in Weaver's case to medieval religion and the chivalrous, patriarchal, anti-egalitarian, presumably nonmaterialist Old South for its source of inspiration and truth. Unlike his free market counterparts, Weaver truly did see the rise of rational empirical inquiry as the beginning of what he memorably called, and dated to the fourteenth century, the "dissolution of the West." As an approach to knowledge, an appeal to the romance of lost causes, and especially as a strategy for the still-hoped-for restoration of conservative principles, *Ideas Have Consequences* operated and continues to operate as something of a rallying and unifying point within the movement. The sanctity of private property, Weaver acknowledged, was an idea that conservatives of all stripes could agree on. But so, too, was the idea that the importance of knowledge was not in facts and contingent values but in transcendent virtues and eternal truth.[42] This appeal to truth, to an order of knowledge that is basically impervious to empirical argumentation, is what movement intellectuals refer to in framing their cause as a battle of ideas. This is one reason why responding to that knowledge with facts and evidence of inconsistency can go only so far. For the time being, however, the prevailing liberal response was not to respond at all. In the logic of a dominant, ideology-ending consensus, there was no need to.

Conservative activists, meanwhile, would keep these ideas circulating within the right-wing public sphere. They would do so in publications such as *Human Events, Encounter, the Freeman*, and, beginning in 1955, in William F. Buckley's *National Review*, whose editors would position the magazine as a venue for defining conservatism as an internally conflicted, yet potentially unified ideological movement. "Fusionist" was the term that *National Review* editor Frank Meyer used. Ideas of traditionalist and free market conservatives coincided and sometimes clashed on its pages. More often, however, they found common ground, in anticommunism, in resistance to change (which included civil rights), and above all in opposition to the liberal establishment and all it stood for. Along with dedicated political operatives such as Goldwater acolyte Phyllis Schlafly, *National Review* devoted a good deal of ink to exposing the existence of this nefarious establishment, bound together by the dogmas of Keynesianism, philosophical pragmatism, and ideology-ending social scientific empiricism. As Meyer wrote in a 1958 column:

> So long as the Establishment that is inspired by this view is in the ascendancy, there are only two historical alternatives: that our civilization will be destroyed from within, by the gradual triumph of the regnant anti-Western principle; or that it will be destroyed from without by Communist conquest, against which the votaries of this destructive relativist principle have in the end no defense, having no rock of ultimate defiance upon which to stand against Communism.[43]

Ultimately, however, the power to dethrone the liberal social scientific establishment would come from the convergence not of otherwise disparate ideas but of otherwise disparate political mobilizations—one grass roots and populist, the other elite, but both, as discussed in the following chapters, dedicated to reviving, recapturing and ultimately to redefining the social question to restore values long eclipsed in the politics of liberal consensus.

❧ CHAPTER 4 ❧

THE POOR LAW, THE SOCIAL QUESTION, AND THE NEW POLITICS OF REFORM

When conservatives tell the story of counterrevolution, two themes invariably loom large. One is the moral failure of liberalism. The other is the power of conservative ideas. Nowhere do they come together more powerfully than in the story conservative intellectuals tell about the book that brought about the counterrevolution in welfare, Charles Murray's *Losing Ground* (1984).[1]

In the now legendary annals of counterrevolutionary triumph, the story begins with Murray as an obscure scholar toiling away at an equally obscure think tank known to only a very few as the Manhattan Institute, both on the verge of a major social policy breakthrough. He is a lone, clear-eyed numbers-cruncher, challenging a hopelessly liberal research establishment. Daring to think the unthinkable, he comes to the reams of social scientific data with a new set of questions and no stake in what the numbers reveal. What he learns is nevertheless a stunning revelation that smashes conventional wisdom. Welfare, not poverty, was the problem. Lyndon B. Johnson's War on Poverty had actually made poverty more pathological, self-perpetuating, and entrenched. All this could be told through the (basically flawed, as critics showed) statistical correlations, but it was the story behind the numbers that no one else had ever dared tell. Liberals had set the poverty pathology in motion in exactly 1964, with morally permissive policies that blamed the system, undermined individual responsibility and self-reliance, and effectively created incentives for poor people to choose unemployment, single motherhood, and welfare rather than subject themselves to the natural discipline of the low-wage workforce. Murray told this story in what would become a famous "thought experiment" involving a mythical couple named Phyllis and George. It was with such pithy policy stories, legend has it, and with the help of a scrappy publicity effort that Charles Murray is said to have changed the conversation overnight. Those, and Murray's startling conclusion—end welfare, and with it the scourge that the permissive liberal welfare state had visited on the poor.[2]

As an object lesson in the post–liberal politics of knowledge, the story of Murray's book does highlight important themes. *Losing Ground* did cause a major stir in policy circles and did establish Murray and his Manhattan Institute sponsors as figures to be reckoned with. It did help to make ending welfare a part of the policy conversation, even if as the unimaginably radical, mean-spirited right-wing extreme.[3] It did reflect the conscious and explicit injection of ideology into expertise that would become a hallmark of the right-wing "advocacy tanks."[4] The story has also been thoroughly absorbed into conservative movement culture, where Murray's book provides the proof that ideas do have consequences. One recent publication, using it to punctuate the point, referred to *Losing Ground* as a "bible of sorts for reformers in the Reagan and Bush Administrations."[5]

As the story of conservatism's capture of the welfare issue, however, the heroic saga of *Losing Ground* is as basically flawed as Murray's statistical analysis turned out to be. For one thing, Murray was hardly a voice in the political wilderness and *Losing Ground* was hardly based on a new idea. Indeed, it was based on questions endlessly asked and answered over two centuries of poor law reform.[6] Does welfare make poor people lazy and idle and begging for more? Does it enable the poor to breed without suffering the natural consequences of hunger and privation? Most recently, they had been asked and for all intents and purposes answered in the populist antiwelfare politics of the newly resurgent conservative right. *Losing Ground*, then, owed its success not to a brilliant insight, and not merely to a brilliant public relations effort, but as well to the larger conservative movement and to its ability, with growing momentum in the 1970s and 1980s, to gain control of and reframe the essential terms of the social question, and from there of the welfare debate. Murray, of course, was identifiably a part of that movement as an intellectual and a fellow of Antony Fisher's free market Manhattan Institute. The ground he stood on, however, was as firmly based in electoral, and reform, and especially in movement-building politics as in the more esoteric politics of ideas. The more essential work of recapturing and reframing the debate had been underway for more than a decade. Furthermore, the movement that made Charles Murray's success possible was as deeply invested in gaining, and keeping, political power as it was in the power of ideas.

It is to illuminate what made *Losing Ground* such a galvanizing intervention that I turn briefly away from social science and philanthropy to the deeper politics of the social question as played out in the unexpectedly template-setting blueprint for welfare reform set in motion by then Governor Ronald Reagan in 1970s California. My aim is not to retell the complicated story of welfare reform but to draw attention to two developments in late twentieth-century social politics that would prove critical to making the conservative counterrevolution of ideas possible.

First was the way activists were able to use welfare reform as a defining issue for the disparate strands of new and old right activism then just beginning to mobilize into a unified electoral constituency. In this broader mobilization, welfare reform served not only as a unifying, galvanizing issue but also as a kind of template for the distinctively right-wing, aggressively antiliberal style of reform politics that—later embodied in such manifestos as the *Contract with America* (1994)—would catapult the Republican right from the radical fringe of opposition to the party of domestic policy reform.

Second was the blueprint that Reagan's campaign against welfare offered for capturing and reframing the social question in a way that effectively disarmed the neutral expertise of the poverty research establishment. Here, Reagan's initiative can be seen as but one part of a concerted, ultimately successful campaign among right-wing activists to capture welfare reform as a political issue starting in the early 1970s. The initiative, however, also helped to make welfare a kind of template for a wider array of domestic social issues—poverty, the urban crisis, law and order, and especially race—that would similarly be reframed as part of a remoralized social question holding liberal permissiveness to blame. As conservatives knew all too well at the time, capturing the welfare reform issue was no easy or obvious task. Among other things, it would require a massive reorientation of the nationalizing, standardizing reform logic then coming from Washington and endorsed by a widening cadre of experts, including moderates within the Republican Party. It would also entail redefining the welfare crisis—and indeed the broader social question—in the explicitly ideological, moralistic tones that had long since come to be regarded as anachronistic in Washington policy-making circles. Most daunting of all from the perspective of the early 1970s, when there was no Heritage Foundation, Cato, or Manhattan Institute to rival the likes of the Brookings Institution or the Urban Institute or the still-expanding array of federal government policy analytic shops, it would require wresting control of the social policy conversation from the entrenched, institutionalized, and interlocking if not conspiratorial liberal policy establishment that had come to dominate the terms of debate.

In 1971, California mounted an overhaul of its public assistance programs, one of several local-, state-, and national-level responses to a so-called welfare crisis that had led to rapid growth in welfare costs and enrollments over the previous decade.[7] Based on a controversial and only partially successful legislative package that Governor Ronald Reagan had proposed, the plan was later featured as California's pioneering blueprint for national welfare reform in a pamphlet issued by the governor's office and circulated to national policy makers in 1974 and 1975.[8] By then, Congress had already been through a long series of bruising battles over competing plans for comprehensive federal welfare reform. Very much at the center of these battles was President Richard M. Nixon's twice-failed proposal to replace welfare with a minimum income guarantee program called the Family Assistance Plan (FAP). By extending benefits to two-parent families and a broader segment of the low-wage working class, FAP would have significantly expanded both the ranks of income support recipients and the role of the federal government in financing and regulating state-administered public assistance. In this more expansive, federalizing direction, FAP also reflected what had become a widely shared, if fragile, agreement among the otherwise divided group of policy intellectuals, social welfare practitioners, state and local officials, and welfare rights activists who had provided the momentum for a series of welfare reform measures since the late 1950s. The old Aid to Dependent Children program, recently revised and renamed Aid to Families with Dependent Children (AFDC), was inefficient, unfair, and inadequate as an antipoverty measure.[9] For all the crisis mongering that attended discussion of the seemingly inexorable growth of the existing welfare rolls, the prevailing sentiment among inside-the-Beltway experts was that the system need be made more fair, uniform, and, for whatever mixture of motives, responsive to the needs of the working poor.[10]

This, overwhelmingly, was the welfare reform consensus of the broadly social scientific establishment. It was backed by the kind of neutral expertise that made the coming of some kind of universalizing welfare reform, however briefly, seem as close as anything in Washington to being inevitable. Liberal proponents of a basic guaranteed income could point to no less a conservative figure than Milton Friedman as an ally. Albeit for very different reasons, Friedman had endorsed the idea in principle.[11]

California's Blueprint for National Welfare Reform offered a decidedly different vision and rationale. It was rooted in a store of ideas that, in their frank and unapologetic appeal to morality, boldly defied the expertise. It proposed a way to get the federal government to step aside, freeing up the states and localities to do what Reagan was eager to establish as the job of "real" welfare reform. To provide public assistance only to a narrowly defined group of deserving and "truly needy" poor people was one element. To purge the rolls of the presumably large numbers of morally "undeserving" or otherwise unfairly entitled recipients was another. To rid the system of all the "waste, fraud, and abuse" promulgated by greedy recipients and corrupt administrators was a third component. To cre-

ate incentives to leave the system by requiring all able-bodied recipients to work in mandatory community work relief programs in
exchange for benefits was a fourth. To enforce individual and "family responsibility" as the first line of income provision, especially on
the part of absent parents, was a fifth objective. Last was to put a
cap on program growth, largely through issuing fixed sums to the
localities.[12] For all but the legitimately disabled, dependent, or otherwise "deserving," public assistance would be a tightly regulated,
temporary, relatively inexpensive, locally controlled and heavily
stigmatized—if not downright punitive—source of poor relief.
Welfare, in Reagan's plan, would return to the old poor law tradition from which decades of reform, social policy, and (more recently) "permissive" liberal governance had allowed it to stray.

Prescient though it may appear in light of the provisions legislat-
ing the "end of welfare as we know it" in 1996, my concern here is
less with the specifics of the reform vision outlined in Reagan's
blueprint than with its significance in the growing dominance over
the terms of the social question established by the resurgent right.

Issued near the end of his oft-compromised governorship and as
speculation about the 1976 presidential nomination set in, Reagan's
blueprint for reform was inextricably tied to his political ambition
to remain the standard-bearer and the candidate of the right wing
of the Republican Party that had embraced him as its great hope in
the wake of Senator Barry Goldwater's dramatically failed presidential candidacy in 1964. That welfare reform would play a prominent role in the right's hoped-for resurgence was virtually guaranteed—not only by the growth and changing color of the welfare
rolls but also by the tremendous political fallout the bitter debates
over Nixon's FAP had caused. Reagan, using what leverage he had
as governor of the state with the nation's second-largest caseload
and as spokesman for the alienated Republican right, had already
positioned himself as a bulwark against what conservative weekly
Human Events called the reform juggernaut by taking an early, aggressive, and highly public stance against FAP.[13] Announcing his
opposition in press releases, letters to every member of Congress,
and in a nationally televised debate, Reagan in early 1970 appointed a task force to come up with an alternative state reform

plan.[14] He had concluded, "after careful and extensive study," that, among other things, FAP would both add millions to California's welfare rolls and undermine the work ethic.[15] The task force plan—the basis of Reagan's national blueprint—would do just the opposite and at the same time distinguish California as the vanguard of a state-initiated conservative welfare reform movement.[16]

Facing substantial opposition from the Democratic California legislature, Reagan proved equally aggressive about resisting the trends in Washington and placing himself, and the conservative right, in the vanguard of alternative welfare reform. Even while agitating for legislative approval of his controversial plan (which, in addition to tighter eligibility and tougher-than-national work requirements, proposed a co-payment for Medi-Cal, the state Medicaid program), he lobbied Nixon administration officials and congressional allies relentlessly to get approval for the federal waivers that would allow the plan to be implemented. He also took every opportunity he could to lobby through the National Governors Association, both in opposition to FAP and in favor of his waiver request. Here, as in most instances, he positioned himself as the lone and principled resistance to the reformers' liberalizing tide.

Moreover, for all the backlash and counterproposals the FAP debate had galvanized, a plan had yet to emerge that would rival the income guarantee in scope yet bring these disparate strands in conservative welfare activism together. Reagan's California Blueprint attempted to do this, by offering a concrete alternative to the direction of the prevailing comprehensive reform trend and indeed by rejecting the idea of a centrally orchestrated overhaul altogether. Welfare overhaul was necessary, but it was best accomplished incrementally, by the states, with additional waivers from the federal government to allow local officials to get the undeserving off the rolls and put the employables to work, and without such centralized and untried schemes as a guaranteed income. As it turns out, the success Reagan and others claimed based on their efforts in California was highly exaggerated. AFDC rolls did go down in the early 1970s, largely due to the economy and administratively tightened eligibility requirements. Welfare payments did go up for the "truly needy"—largely because California Democrats insisted on indexing payments as one price for passing the reform bill. Reagan's highly controversial community work program, which required recipients to work off their grants, met with wide resistance in localities and in court challenges, and even by Reagan's admission was meant mostly as a symbolic gesture to deter the able-bodied from applying for benefits in the first place.[17]

But if Reagan's blueprint was not exactly remarkable as a plan for fixing welfare, it did hold lasting significance as a political program for the emergent conservative right. For in laying out a distinctively conservative plan for dealing with the welfare crisis, the California Blueprint and the state-based reform effort behind it helped to establish welfare—narrowly defined as cash programs for the poor who were neither elderly nor disabled—as a powerful issue. Around it, the disparate, potentially conflicting strands within right-wing conservatism could organize, both to oppose the excesses of liberal "welfarism" and, equally important, to counter the dominance of the Republican Party's moderate wing. Beyond offering a concrete proposal that could turn conservative opposition to FAP into a positive reform program, Reagan-style reform activism tapped into and crystallized a bundle of resentments and anxieties about core social values and governing principles that resurrected without directly invoking the principles of the Elizabethan poor law. As such, it helped to single out welfare as an issue that, for conservatives especially, could have staying power beyond any immediate legislative victory, to the project of movement-building itself. It is in this sense that the blueprint underscores the political importance of capturing the welfare issue—and through it, the larger social question—to the rise of the conservative right.

Equally important to the politics of the social question, in several respects Reagan's welfare reform can be seen as a harbinger of a still-emerging brand of reform politics that would come to distinguish the conservative right and its use of knowledge. One was in its demonization of AFDC in particular, and more generally cash programs for the younger or able-bodied poor, as the crux of the welfare problem. Of course, right-wing conservatives were hardly alone in singling out AFDC as an exemplar of a widely reported welfare crisis. Well before his (re)incarnation as Nixon's domestic policy adviser, Daniel P. Moynihan had been warning about the "crises" in welfare, pointing to the dramatic rise and growing proportion of single-mother families on the AFDC rolls as a sign of deeper social pathologies. Liberal policy analysts and economists associated with the Great Society, though generally avoiding the rhetoric of crisis, had grown increasingly vociferous about their aggravation with the program's inefficiencies, its categorical nature, and the inequities stemming from vast disparities in benefit standards across states.[18] But targeting AFDC (and, in Reagan's blueprint, food stamps) had a particular significance for the right. For one thing, it provided concreteness and focus for the more generalized anti–welfare state sentiment that, during the post–World War II decades, had distinguished the conservative right from the moderates within the Republican Party. Right-wing intellectuals and activists had long appealed to shared animosity against the New Deal welfare state. They had yet, however, to channel such sentiment into a concerted, targeted, issue-oriented campaign that had much chance of garnering widespread political support. In fact, when Barry Goldwater and later Ronald Reagan attempted to take on Social Security, they were labeled extremists. Moreover, mobilizing animosity to the New Deal welfare state posed a problem that the right was not prepared to confront: the burgeoning middle-class, suburbanized, white constituency to which the right would look for a mass voting base was in many ways the creation of the federal largesse the right denounced.[19] To be sure, Americans have proved perfectly capable of ignoring the conflict between their anti–welfare statism and the degree to which their affluence is subsidized by the welfare state—owing, in no small part, to its design and the hidden nature of its middle-class benefits. Targeting AFDC, however, offered a way to avoid the conflict altogether. It was redistributive, bureaucratic, and socialistic, like the welfare state in general, and it was a program for other people.

As significant as the focus on AFDC was the distinctive way in which the right, as reflected in California's reform plan, was beginning to characterize the nature of the problem its spiraling growth presented. As Reagan emphasized in his foreword to the 1974 blueprint, the issue went well beyond the "dizzying" growth and added costs California was experiencing. AFDC was a "moral and administrative disaster" as well. The "truly needy," he claimed, were being cheated out of the beneficence they deserved because "others were abusing the system by claiming, and getting, benefits they didn't deserve." The taxpayers were being cheated as well, not only by seeing their hard-earned dollars go to the undeserving, but by watching the poor get better services (Medi-Cal and T-bone steaks) than they were able to pay for themselves. AFDC and food stamps were subsidizing rampant bad behavior among undeserving recipients, the blueprint went on to report, but federal administrators and social workers, by encouraging families to take full advantage of overly generous income exemptions, were in on the fix as well.[20] This emphasis on welfare's immorality—of its recipients as well as its scheming bureaucrats—echoed familiar themes of undeservingness and antistatism. It also, however, distinguished them even more sharply from the more generic right-wing anti–welfare state rhetoric of the past. Furthermore, it distinguished the right's diagnosis from other contemporary renditions of the welfare crisis. Even Moynihan, who made his case against welfare by linking it to the rise in single-mother households, framed it as a social problem that required improving provisions for two-parent poor families. For Reagan, who in the blueprint paid far more attention to fraud and abuse than to single parenthood, the immorality was individual and called for punishment. Also, and in contrast to proponents of the guaranteed income, who raised the issue of fairness by pointing out that two-parent working poor families were left out of the system altogether, for Reagan the line between deserving and undeserving had to be drawn far more parsimoniously. The able-bodied, by definition, were not the truly needy. If anything, putting them on welfare had sent them into a downward spiral of dependency and subsidized idleness that had rendered them truly undeserving of public aid.

But in framing welfare as a moral crisis, Reagan had more than individual behavior in mind. He meant to call attention to the immorality of the liberal state. Key to this, and to the larger political momentum of right-wing antiwelfarism, was the link between the crisis in AFDC—a New Deal program—Great Society liberalism, and all the anxieties about social unrest that term conjured up. The blueprint, and the reform initiative it grew out of, accomplished this sleight of hand by blaming welfare's growth on a broader culture of guilt-ridden liberal permissiveness, embodied in a combination of legislative expansion, bureaucratic connivance, and, especially, litigation brought by war on poverty lawyers on behalf of the poor. It also steered conservatism's moral compass to the hitherto relatively unsullied Food Stamp program, which in Reagan's eyes had taken moral and administrative laxity to an even greater extreme. Food stamps, the blueprint reported in anecdotal detail, were subsidizing not only welfare cheaters but strikers (hence the union movement), University of California students living in communes and otherwise rebelling against their parents, and denizens of the ghetto underground. Readers between the lines could see references to the major struggles of Reagan's governorship, here folded in to the more widespread decline of moral authority at the hands of an overly permissive federal state.

To be sure, at the heart of Reagan's right-wing mobilization against welfare was a discourse of undeservingness that played on a whole host of racialized and gendered fears, prejudices, and stereotypes conjured up by the image of the "welfare queen" living high off the benefits of the liberal state. Reagan proved a master at this, later using every possible occasion to tell the widely publicized story about a Chicago "welfare queen" charged with fraud for using "eighty names, thirty addresses, twelve Social Security cards, and . . . four nonexistent deceased husbands" to collect some $150,000 from welfare and the Veterans Administration. In reality, the woman in question had been charged with using four aliases to bilk the system of $8,000, but this did not prevent the candidate from repeating the story throughout the 1976 campaign. Reagan also singled out the tax burden created by welfare support for immigrants and illegal aliens and succeeded in outlawing benefits for illegal immigrants at the state level, suggesting as he did so that California was bearing the burden of lax federal immigration restrictions.

Moreover, this emphasis on the tax burden, like the racialized imagery of welfare cheats, was very much aimed at the white working-class constituency that, as Nixon had well understood in 1968, was very much up for grabs. Nixon, disturbed by the picture of an alienated, struggling "white ethnic" in a welter of media reports, had already identified welfare reform as a way to foment Great Society backlash and to win the allegiance of the "forgotten Americans" he had featured in his campaign. In this, he was at least partly steered by Daniel P. Moynihan, who in the months leading up to Nixon's original announcement of FAP in August 1969 was the most vigorous administration proponent of extending basic income supports to the two-parent families more and more frequently referred to as the working poor. The family allowance was a way to do something for this critical, neglected, potentially growing, and without question deserving group, Moynihan indicated to the president as the internal FAP debate was raging. It is a group, he added, "that cannot logically or humanely be ignored by those who seek to address the problem of black, non-working, abject poverty."[21]

Recognizing welfare reform as a way to tap into the racial resentments of the white working class, right-wing reform activists were equally aggressive in tapping the class resentments of the more established and especially the just-above-poverty working class, playing up welfare's cost to increasingly squeezed taxpayers, and warning that Nixon's plan would only squeeze them more. The "working poor do not need government cash supplements," the American Conservative Union flatly proclaimed in its denunciation of Nixon's FAP, to which the U.S. Chamber of Commerce added its conclusion that "the fellow who is just barely above the cut-off level" for payments would be subsidizing the one who got food stamps while doing the same—or less—work.[22] This alone, as Vice President Spiro Agnew had warned Nixon before the FAP was announced, should prevent the administration from bringing "the addictive philosophy of welfare to those who are presently self-reliant, even if not as comfortable as they would like to be."[23] In sharp contrast to Nixon's FAP, which played hard on the fairness issue but resolved it by extending benefits to the two-parent working poor, Reagan's California reforms—and, in 1981, one of his first and most significant acts as president—singled out the largely unorganized, lowest-wage segment of the working class as undeserving of public benefits. No single group was more severely punished by Reagan's efforts to contain costs and target the truly needy—by (eventually) eliminating income allowances, tightening asset limits, setting work for welfare requirements, and eviscerating training programs—than employed people earning poverty wages. Reagan himself, in his original California proposals and later in the blueprint, pointed to labor regulation as a principal motive for keeping low-wage workers off the welfare rolls. Strikers, he pointed out, in a theme widely echoed by the U.S. Chamber of Commerce, the National Conservative Union, in *Human Events,* and in other right-wing outlets were not prohibited from receiving welfare and food stamps, giving union organizers a way—thanks to the taxpayers—to extend labor walk-outs. What better way to stop it than to include low-wage workers among the undeserving poor?

As we can see from this, welfare—defined narrowly as AFDC and food stamps—could be used as a potent symbol of all that had and was still going wrong in America in the early 1970s and crystallize those problems in an issue, and a set of shorthand images, that lent itself to legislative action. Government was too big, taxes too high, and both were serving the interests of the wrong people. Society was too permissive, coddling not only able-bodied welfare recipients but also the no-account fathers who sired their children and the students who were rebelling against their parents to run off to communes. Federal regulations were thwarting the will of the people and allowing widespread fraud. From the standpoint of a conservative movement made up of several potentially conflicting strands, a crusade against welfare had something for everyone. For social conservatives, reforming welfare would be a stand against out-of-wedlock sexuality and social permissiveness more generally and a stand for family values. For libertarians, it would be a stand against government red tape, self-serving bureaucrats, and the centralized, untried welfare expansion that Nixon, with the help of Washington, D.C.–based poverty experts, had cooked up. For the taxpayers of California, it would be a blow against waste, fraud, and abuse as well as a way to make both government and welfare recipients morally accountable.

Thus, as much as Reagan's California Blueprint did to make welfare a lightening rod for conservative discontent, it is also significant for its efforts to position right-wing conservatives as the agents of real reform, and with that, to redefine the very notion, and aims, of reform. The notion of "real," practical reform in welfare—what Martin Anderson later referred to as "workable reform"—played heavily on the "dismal record" of Nixon's FAP and other such attempts to achieve radical change. Advocates of real reform, by contrast, rejected the idea of radical innovation in favor of a return to what they imagined to be welfare's original, appropriate intent: to provide assistance to the truly needy while upholding the value of self-support.[24] Advocates of real reform looked first to what could be done administratively, as California had managed by tightening up eligibility and cracking down on fraud. Real reform could not start in Washington—Washington, in fact, was part of the problem—but in the states. Real reform was antireformist, especially in the context of the more established tradition of liberal and, now, moderate Republican reform. And California, as Reagan's blueprint outlined and both a small cadre of conservative activists and Reagan himself never tired of pointing out, was the harbinger of a rising movement—a people's movement, even—for real reform in welfare. The Reagan administration, he reported in both the blueprint and campaign speeches, was able to pass welfare reform in California only after going around recalcitrant legislators to appeal to the citizens of California. In testimony before the Senate Finance Committee, Reagan talked about a citizens' organization called Cheaters, made up of angry taxpayers who set out to prove how easy it was to cheat the system. In the citizens' press conferences that became a feature of Reagan's 1976 campaign, villainous stories of welfare cheats were coupled with heroic stories of the people coming together to put a stop to fraud.

Linked to this populist appeal was Reagan's basic contempt for the whole apparatus of welfare and its regulation, a contempt he would continually reinforce in placing morally corrupt bureaucrats at the center of the welfare crisis. This did not prevent him from using that apparatus to undermine the liberal welfare state. Nowhere was this more evident than in the concerted right-wing campaign

115

to create a far-reaching counterintelligentsia of academics and policy intellectuals to wage ideological warfare against the liberal welfare state, a campaign that would cultivate policy intellectuals such as Charles Murray and one I discuss in greater detail in chapter 5. Reagan's welfare reform blueprint, which preceded that countermobilization, nevertheless anticipated two of its defining features. One was its reliance on a combination of anecdote and cultural narrative, in sharp contrast to the heavily statistical, rigorously empirical style of mainstream policy analysis. The other was its willingness, in a realm organized on a putatively nonideological ethos, to use knowledge as an ideological and movement-building force. As played out most fully in the policy briefs of the Heritage Foundation and in Murray's *Losing Ground*, this style of policy analysis would eventually adopt the conventions of neutral expertise to illustrate the perverse incentives and basic immorality of the liberal welfare state. Murray, of course, was not the first or the only analyst to point out that some rationally calculating people might find that they would be better off on welfare than working at a minimum wage job. People remembered George and Phyllis, however, as well as Murray's draconian conclusion. The welfare debate, in turn, only reinforced the growing recognition among conservative activists that they were operating at a distinct disadvantage in Washington, precisely because they did not have the analytic apparatus—or the institutional network to produce it—to take on the liberal-moderate leaning think tank and administrative policy establishment.

In every which way, then, Reagan's blueprint for welfare reform was anathema to the nominally neutral policy research establishment that—well after the Nixon administration abandoned FAP—continued to endorse some form of more centralized and streamlined basic income approach to reform. More fundamentally at odds, though, was the idiom of morality, need, and undeservingness through which Reagan entered that would more and more come to dominate the distinctively moralized social policy debate.

By the time Charles Murray entered the poor law debate with his "conversation-changing" book, Ronald Reagan was looking forward to his second term in office, and the basic terms of the conversation had long since been set. Although nothing approaching "ending welfare" was on the table, a great deal was being accomplished incrementally and behind the scenes. Thus, when Reagan was in a position to implement his blueprint, he achieved far more under the cover of budget cutbacks and changes in administrative rules than in anything that could be labeled comprehensive reform. All expectations to the contrary, he did not launch a concerted initiative on assuming the presidency in 1981. The welfare reform task force created in the aftermath of the 1986 State of the Union address was something of an afterthought, though it did generate a proliferation of complementary and competing task forces, and eventually led to the Family Support Act of 1988. By then, however, much of the blueprint was already in place. Thanks to the aggressive budget cuts and regulations introduced in the Omnibus Budget Reconciliation Act of 1981, welfare eligibility was more than ever confined to the very lowest income earners (effectively removing the working poor from welfare eligibility), Community Work Experience Programs (work for welfare benefits) were written into federal regulations, the states were encouraged to make more aggressive use of waivers from federal regulations, and services were cut to the bone. As it turns out, then, and ironically, the most sweeping, indeed comprehensive, welfare overhaul since 1935 was made possible by the comparatively incremental steps taken to pave the way—starting with the basic reformulation of the social question Reagan's blueprint and the movement surrounding it had put in play.

What made Charles Murray's *Losing Ground* a galvanizing intervention was thus neither the originality nor the inherent power of its idea. It was that Murray joined a conversation long since thoroughly reshaped and remoralized along the lines of the Malthusian logic the book would deploy. It was a conversation that Murray and others were joining from institutions that, to a greater degree and in larger numbers than ever before, were being organized for conservative ideological purposes and along conservative ideological lines. It was also a conversation to which they would bring both the apparatus of neutral social science and the determination to use it for the conservative cause.

117

❧ CHAPTER 5 ❧

THE COUNTERINTELLIGENTSIA, THE SOCIAL QUESTION, AND THE NEW GOSPEL OF WEALTH

Ultimately, it was a different kind of political mobilization that channeled right-wing issue revolts in such incendiary areas as welfare, taxes, and race into a more sustained ideological counter-revolution, and that took on the liberal social scientific establishment in a full-scale ideological counterattack. Although building on and steeped in the same bundle of values and animosities fueling grassroots opposition to liberal "welfarism," this was very much, and very deliberately, a "revolt of the elites."[1] It rested on the activism not so much of populist politicians appealing to the working and middle classes, but instead of conservative intellectuals and business executives. The venue they created was a mirror image of the executive suites, think tanks, university classrooms, and foundation boardrooms that populists had long viewed skeptically. It relied heavily, though not by any means exclusively, on a self-consciously countermobilization of private philanthropic wealth.

The aim of this mobilization was an ambition that presented itself as a new Gospel of Wealth, to align philanthropic wealth with the interests of corporate and free market capitalism, and indeed to establish those interests as expressions of both private virtue and the public good. Convinced that the great fortunes of early twentieth-century industrial capitalism were irreversibly controlled by an anticapitalist liberal elite, the new philanthropic activists would organize to break or at least to counter that stranglehold in an alter-

118

native network of foundations. In a tightly focused strategy that emphasized funding for conservative individuals, institutions, and ideas, the leading conservative foundations set out to launch the counterrevolution long envisioned in such intellectual outposts as the Mont Pelerin Society—this time in earnest and this time with results. Their goal was at once sweepingly ambitious and avowedly conservative. They wanted to recapture not only the social question but American politics and political culture writ large as well. They intended to do so by establishing limited government, free enterprise, and individualism as prevailing political norms. That they have been substantially successful with enormous but still comparatively limited assets has been a point of pride for their leading spokesmen and of puzzlement for their critics. It is principally attributable to the fact that the conservative foundations have been self-consciously part of a broader political movement. In this movement, they represent only a portion of the financial resources but have nonetheless provided critical "venture capital" for the think tanks, university-based research institutes, publications, professional societies, media outlets, and policy advocacy organizations that have been the counterrevolution's mainstay. Prominent among them were the foundations that, as of the late 1990s, have gained considerable notoriety as the source of the funding that brought us what has been viewed as an "axis of ideology" in recognition of their collective importance as right-wing movement philanthropy: the Lynde and Harry Bradley, Earhart, Koch Family, Smith-Richardson, Sarah Scaife, Coors, JM, and the John M. Olin foundations.[2]

More than as simply the deep pockets of the movement, these and similarly inclined foundations have also been singled out for what makes them, in sharp contrast to their liberal counterparts, so effective in shaping and steering the outcomes of significant policy debates. First is a willingness to fund institutions with unrestricted and infrastructural rather than project-by-project grants, and to fund over the long term, again with large untethered grants. Second is an emphasis on core ideas over empirical research. Third is a coordinated strategy of network-building that moves from the local to the national and global and from think tank to public sphere. Fourth, of course, is an unapologetic commitment to a conservative political and ideological agenda, however orchestrated within the boundaries of what tax exempt status demands.

But more significant in understanding the nature of this mobilization and its significance for the liberal tradition it aims to rival were three things that came together in the 1970s and 1980s to differentiate this generation of conservative foundations from their postwar predecessors and to transform what had been scattered, isolated efforts into a full-throttled philanthropic movement with long-lasting effects.

One was the central role played by that highly problematic, increasingly controversial group of intellectuals known as neoconservatives, those once-stalwart, now deeply disillusioned former democratic socialists, left-, and consensus liberals who by the early 1970s were turning their energies to the conservative cause. The neoconservatives were suspect to many within the movement—as relative newcomers, as unredeemed statists, as still-registered Democrats, and in some quarters as a group originally and most commonly identified with a cluster of New York Jewish intellectuals. Nevertheless leading neoconservative figures such as Irving Kristol, Nathan Glazer, Norman Podhoretz, Midge Decter, Michael Novak, James Q. Wilson, William Bennett, Jeane Kirkpatrick, and for a brief time Daniel Patrick Moynihan were becoming increasingly prominent in framing the disparate strands within postwar conservatism as a unified, if internally contentious, movement of ideas. Here, notably, they were acting not as original thinkers but more as publicists, brokers, and revivalists of ideas and political philosophies not long ago dismissed as anathema to modern liberal democracy. In this capacity, neoconservatives would serve as legitimizers for ideas they may once have rejected but now embraced with the authenticity of the disillusioned realist (Irving Kristol's "liberal who has been mugged by reality") if not always the zeal of the newly converted (Kristol, again, mustering only "Two Cheers for Capitalism").[3]

As former left-liberals, the neoconservatives also brought an element of authority to the critique of liberalism, presenting themselves as the true liberal idealists who had in some fashion or another actually experienced or even been victimized by liberalism's illusions or by its alleged takeover by radical extremists. (How often are we reminded that Charles Murray was once a Peace Corps volunteer, or that anti-affirmative action activists marched with Martin Luther King at Selma?) Equally important, and especially on the pages of such initially iconoclastic, then conservative journals as Kristol (et al.'s) *The Public Interest*, the neoconservatives brought the authority of empirical social science to the conservative project. Now, though, they used it to erode rather than to reaffirm liberal faiths. Indeed, in their earliest critiques the first generation of neoconservatives was steeped in the consciousness of the postwar liberal consensus. It was from within its bastions—the expanding universities, the analytic think tanks, the cold war cultural front, the journals of elite opinion—that many would begin their journey to the right. But the generational experience that most dramatically galvanized the neoconservatives was the experience of the 1960s, which found many of them on the "wrong" side of campus protest and countercultural experimentation, embittered by what they saw as liberalism's capitulation to radical civil rights demands. It was thus with a sense of having been betrayed by the promise of liberalism that they would join with conservative movement activists to garner knowledge and philanthropy for the conservative cause.

A second factor was the coalescence of political interests reflected in an emerging alliance between an increasingly organized, CEO-dominated segment of the business class and a growing cadre of conservative New Class intellectuals. Unlikely in several respects, this alliance aimed to do for the pro-capitalist, deregulatory, free market lobby what conservatives thought Ralph Nader and liberal foundations had done for their consumerist-environmentalist-public interest opponents. It would establish the professionalized associational infrastructure for representing capitalism and its interests in government agencies, legislative affairs, and especially in the courts. The business-intellectual alliance was also based on the proposition that not only capitalism but also the spirit of capitalism was in peril from the regulations, the labor and consumer protections, and more generally the collectivist impulses of the so-called campus radicals and the liberal state. The movement to ener-

121

gize pro-capitalist, pro-business philanthropy was a powerful expression of this newfound business-intellectual alliance. It was a dimension of a more sweeping countermobilization that would come to target the media, the opinion, political advertising, and publishing industries, and the infamous K Street corridor as well. But it was an important dimension, especially in targeting what conservative intellectuals had long considered the fulcrum of liberal establishment power: its hitherto unchallenged monopoly over the institutions of knowledge and culture and, through them, over political discourse.

The third factor was timing, along with an idea that conservative philosophers have spent a great deal of time critiquing, historical contingency. Like the larger movement it was part of, the concerted effort to mobilize conservative philanthropy gained momentum amidst and consciously played off the cascading crises of postwar liberalism. To the crises indelibly associated with the 1960s—the welfare and urban crises, the stalled and ever-volatile struggles for racial justice, the deepening alienation from government, the debacle of Vietnam and the polarized reaction on the homefront—could now be added the recurrent oil, inflation, and fiscal crises of the 1970s that came powerfully to symbolize the end of postwar affluence at home and the American Century abroad. It was a time when the problems before the polity simply could not be explained, let alone addressed, within the framework of the Keynesian, pluralist consensus, yet when neither liberalism nor a neutralized social science seemed prepared to engage the questions of state, society, the market, and especially not of ideology and public philosophy those crises raised.

It was also a moment of vulnerability and uncertainty within the established philanthropic sector. This mood was prompted as much by the times as by a combination of recession-diminished resources, skittishness about recently instituted federal regulations, and enduring political fallout from the movement activism the most prominent foundations had momentarily embraced in the 1960s.[4] Although RSF remained comparatively immune to the direct charges of liberal activism and continued to occupy its place on the "second trench," the more generalized mood of uncertainty was captured in an influential essay co-authored by RSF board President Aaron Wildavsky with staff member James A. Douglas, and published in the 1976–1977 annual report. Titled *The Knowledgeable Foundation*, it traced the source of foundation malaise principally to the growth of government and its assumption of philanthropy's once-useful function. But the essay also pointed to the corrosive influence of a more pervasive skepticism about what public policy could achieve. What foundations needed, Douglas and Wildavsky wrote, was a "new intellectual rationale," to shift from their former preoccupation with the consequences of "market failure" to more systematic consideration of what happened when government failed.[5]

Within this general mood of drift, the moment was ripe for a philanthropic activism that was anything but uncertain on the matter of government failure and crystal clear about the need to reassert individual freedom, property rights, hard-line anticommunism, moral traditionalism, and an opposition to liberal statism as core American values. In this sense of clarity, purpose, and direction, the new philanthropic activism was to some degree an agent but as well a harbinger of major shifts: the subordination of the state and civil society to the private market in political economy as in public philosophy, the political erosion of the idea that there is a difference between private wealth and the public interest, and the profound and explicit shift in the direction of redistributive policy to favor the interests of wealth, property, and capital over those of work, wages, and labor.[6]

This, then, and not simply its strategic acumen, is the challenge the rise of conservative movement philanthropy poses to foundations that position themselves as neutral in a polity that has shifted quite dramatically to the right. The movement has succeeded as part of a now-dominant conservatism whose very purpose has been to invalidate just about every precept of the liberal philanthropic project, from the notion of an independent public interest to the notion that there is a public interest in reducing market inequities. The question then becomes whether it is possible to do the work of liberal philanthropy without challenging the assumptions of what has become the dominant public philosophy.

As discussed, and as figures from Hayek and Friedman to Goldwater and Reagan had anticipated, the concerted effort toward conservative counterrevolution would start with redefining the social question. More precisely, it would start with redefining a series of especially volatile social problems as crises wrought by liberal ideology and culture and by the "special interests" liberalism embraced. By the early 1970s, catalyzed by the potent combination of "social revolution," cold war reversals, and the end of affluence, conservative intellectuals were beginning to merge these varied reframings into a narrative of liberal failure and moral corruption. Of particular significance for the effort to mobilize the philanthropic right, they cultivated a critique of the foundation-funded liberal establishment that, minus the more overt anti-intellectualism of earlier right-wing critics, brought a degree of hitherto elusive respectability to older, McCarthy-era charges of creeping collectivism, cultural relativism, and liberal elitism. To these charges conservative ideologues added a broader analysis linking the pillars of liberal thought and policy—Keynesianism, welfare statism, regulation—to economic and cultural decline.

But even more than a common analysis of the country's social and economic woes, three core ideas animated business executives and intellectuals behind the effort to mobilize conservative philanthropic activism. Drawn from long-standing conservative themes, these ideals would now be crystallized into organizing strategies. With them, conservatives would embark on a program of counter-organizing and institution-building that was designed at once to learn from, rival, and ultimately defeat the liberal establishment at its own game.[7]

One took off from Joseph Schumpeter's adage about the source and inevitability of capitalism's demise, joining it to a critique of the concept of the New Class to turn both on their heads. Schumpeter, recall, had written that it was Marx who should be turned on his head. Capitalism, Schumpeter argued, sowed the seeds of its own destruction not by immiserating the proletariat but by creating a class of bourgeois intellectuals who would attack and ultimately undermine its greatest asset, the individualistic, entrepreneurial, creatively destructive competitive edge. The concept of the New

Class, on the other hand, was initially attached to a vision of the postcapitalist future that was considerably more benign.[8] An admittedly vague and elastic concept to start with, it initially aimed to capture what prognosticators of the postindustrial economy saw as an inevitable shift of cultural and political power, away from capitalists to knowledge professionals and, in the more idealistic hopes of a John Kenneth Galbraith, to artists and intellectuals as the vanguard of a more educated, less materialistic, more public-spirited society. It would be married to the Schumpeterian vision in the hands of neoconservatives, however, and mean something slightly different. For them, it came to refer to the intellectuals, the government bureaucrats, the teachers, the foundation and media professionals—all presumably innocent of the nuts and bolts of capitalist enterprise—who promulgated an antibusiness bias not simply as a matter of predisposition or ideology but as a matter of craven self-interest rooted in their incompetence.[9]

This was the point of what became the classically contemptuous formulation of the concept on the right, a 1975 *Wall Street Journal* column by Irving Kristol, "Business and the New Class." Members of the new class, Kristol argued with a keen eye for his readership, were hostile to business in part because they could not make it in business themselves. But they were also hungry for the power that, in a capitalist society, "is supposed to reside in the free market": the power "to shape our civilization." Thus, in claiming to represent the public interest, social scientists, foundation professionals and other denizens of the liberal new class were effectively promulgating a lie. What they really wanted was to aggrandize their own importance—and their subversive values—at capitalism's expense.[10]

There was another twist to Schumpeter's original formulation, one that Kristol and other leading movement intellectuals would make the basis of a strategy to defy Schumpeter's prediction by creating a new class devoted to upholding the values and shoring up the cultural underpinnings of capitalism. That was the idea that capitalists, in creating the material conditions for a thriving university culture, were basically underwriting the class that would bring them down. For Kristol, as for the economist Milton Friedman, the basic truth of this irony was nowhere more evident than in corporate and foundation philanthropy. Friedman, not surprisingly, shared Kristol's contempt for the New Class, and especially for the intellectuals and professionals who populated government and foundation bureaucracies and who embraced a "statist, interventionist philosophy" that had become the basis of their livelihood. This was a self-interest, he added, that "has been reinforced by the herdlike instinct of so many intellectuals. . . to reinforce their prejudices and know little of the other side." Still worse, in continuing to tolerate, even support, their activities through tax dollars and philanthropy, business executives were contributing to capitalism's demise. Yet, Friedman went on, anticipating where New Class analysis could be translated into conservative action, a small but growing segment of intellectuals "have come to recognize the threat that growing government offers to a preservation of human freedom."[11] The challenge was to link these freedom-loving, anti-statist intellectuals with the fervent practitioners of free enterprise in the business world.

That was where the second core idea behind conservative philanthropic activism would come into play. It was often traced to a now-famous memorandum written by Justice Lewis Powell to the U.S. Chamber of Commerce just months before his 1971 appointment to the Supreme Court.[12] Warning of an "assault on the enterprise system" stemming from the likes of Ralph Nader, Charles Reich, Herbert Marcuse, and what he depicted as an overwhelmingly left-liberal bias on campuses and in the media, he called on the chamber to end its practice of "appeasement" by cultivating its own "faculty of scholars" to produce and disseminate pro-business scholarship; creating a network of business interest law firms to combat the public interest law movement; and convincing universities to do more to represent the virtues of capitalism.[13] In fact, the Powell memo picked up on what had already become a steady drumbeat in the right-wing opinion journals and would subsequently be taken up by such prominent business executives as Hewlett-Packard CEO David Packard. In a speech to fellow corporate philanthropists that later made the headlines, Packard argued that business needed to combat the anticapitalist bias on campuses and in the broader culture by funding "the right kind of professors."[14] Packard was to be a major donor to conservative politics and to think tanks such as the Hoover Institute and the American Enterprise Institute. Later on, ironically, his foundation would be used as an object lesson in the perils of allowing liberal do-gooders to hijack original donor intent.[15]

But it was arch-conservative Wall Street executive and Nixon-Ford Treasury Secretary William E. Simon who articulated the idea more fully, publicly, and more directly as a philanthropic project in his aggressively antiliberal manifesto, *A Time for Truth*. Based on lengthy transcribed interviews with ghostwriter Edith Efron, author of *The News-Twisters*, among other popular conservative polemics, the book was written as Simon was finishing his combined stints at Treasury and as Nixon's energy czar. It was organized as a relentless litany of the many liberal "disasters" and "dictatorships" he had witnessed in government, but also as a blueprint for change. The key, he argued with reference to Kristol and others, was to create a conservative counterintelligentsia to protect against the "dominant socialist-statist-collectivist orthodoxy" reigning in universities, government agencies, and policy institutes, and in the philanthropies that funded them.[16] Calling on business, conservative activists, and intellectuals to come to the aid of liberty, Simon envisioned "foundations imbued with the philosophy of freedom" at the forefront of a movement to reestablish capitalism and limited government as the reigning orthodoxy, above all by giving "grants, grants, and more grants in exchange for books, books and more books." Such a project, Simon recognized, could not occur by working from within what had become the philanthropic mainstream. It would require a new kind of foundation and a deliberately orchestrated countermobilization. It would also require a fundamental shift in the very philosophy of philanthropy that, in Simon's view, had animated the liberal establishment's appropriation of capitalist wealth. No longer could business afford to subsidize the critics of capitalism lurking within the halls of academic and public policy institutions. No longer should business apologize for what it was best at, the accumulation of wealth. No longer should the captains of capitalism tolerate the philanthropic appeasement of the enemy by allowing the fruits of their enterprises to be channeled to soft-hearted liberal projects and dissent.[17] That was where Simon's strategy for the counterintelligentsia would meet Friedman's hopes for a conservative new class—hopes Friedman expressed in the preface to Simon's book—in a new generation of foundations dedicated to funding the counterrevolution of ideas.

In opening *A Time for Truth* with tributes from such recognized conservative luminaries as the Nobel Laureate economists Friedman and F. A. Hayek, Simon anchored the business-intellectual alliance to the same tradition of classical liberal economics that had created common cause among free market conservatives throughout the post–World War II years and was continually revisited at annual meetings of the Mont Pelerin Society, to which Simon subscribed. Indeed, Hayek, in handwritten fan mail to Simon, congratulated him on the "fullness of your comprehension of the problems and dangers of current political developments," and went on in his July 4, 1977, foreword to commend the book to "my fellow economists who could learn much from it never dreamed of in their philosophy."[18]

It was the neoconservatives, however, who, as the entrepreneurs and eventually the program officers as well as the grant recipients of the conservative philanthropic project, sustained the momentum behind its third animating idea. This was to make conservative ideology relevant as a political and policy program by framing issues in starkly ideological terms, as failures of liberalism, to be sure, but more and more as clashes of values and culture, even of civilizations—in short, as a war of ideas. The neoconservatives, as Simon saw it, had "grasped the importance of capitalism" in their growing recognition of the dangers of communism, liberal interventionism, and egalitarianism. They also, however, embraced the importance of traditional religious values and moral virtue and would readily invoke them in contemporary political debate. Simon himself was a bridging figure as a devoutly traditional Catholic and a free market devotee. Along with the neoconservative Catholic writer Michael Novak, he would lead an aggressive, largely successful effort to preempt the U.S. Catholic Bishops' 1986 Pastoral Letter on the Economy, a publication titled *Economic Justice for All*. Taking advantage of the lengthy process of public hearings and multiple drafts the bishops traditionally followed, Simon and Novak organized a lay commission of prominent Catholic conservatives to issue its own public letter in advance. In that highly publicized, strategically marketed document, they argued for the basic compatibility between Catholic teaching and free market, growth-oriented economic policy. By the time the bishops were able to issue the first draft of their letter, the media was prepared to report economic justice as a left-leaning, if not minority perspective.[19]

It was the neoconservatives, however, who positioned themselves to bring intellectual heft to the uneasy marriage between free market capitalism and moral traditionalism. For this, they would rely not only on the more familiar ideas of Hayek and Friedman but also on reviving such once-obscure, and often described as obscurantist, proponents of natural rights philosophy as Leo Strauss—whose legacy to a whole generation of neoconservative policy intellectuals would be in justifying the use of state power for moral purposes. It was in this sort of hybrid positioning among competing ideas that the neoconservatives would find their niche within the movement. They would find another in the nonacademic venues of the opinion journals, publishing houses, think tanks, and the conservative foundations.[20] By the late 1970s, it was becoming clear that the neoconservatives were to be the entrepreneurs of conservative policy as well as ideas when they began to join their more traditional counterparts in newly invigorated conservative institutions such as the American Enterprise Institute, to appear with greater frequency in the pages of traditionally liberal journals like *The New Republic* and the *Atlantic,* and on occasion to hobnob with politicians in the corridors of government power.[21]

No single figure captures this combination of intellectual mission and entrepreneurship better than Irving Kristol, the recognized "godfather" of neoconservatism. In large part because of his wide-ranging connections in publishing, conservative politics, and think tanks such as the Heritage Foundation, Hoover Institute, and the American Enterprise Institute (where he was a resident fellow), he has been credited with brokering the connections that brought the Laffer Curve and supply-side economics to the attention of *Wall Street Journal* editorialist Jude Wanniski, thence to the offices of

129

Congressman Jack Kemp, and ultimately to the Reagan White House.[22] Kristol was also, as one of the major promulgators of the anti–New Class polemic in his *Wall Street Journal* columns, ideally situated to broker the relationship between neoconservative intellectuals and the business elite.[23] Equally important, Kristol also became something of an impresario for a group of younger neoconservative idea brokers who would assume key positions on the comparatively smaller and less bureaucratized staffs of the conservative foundations.

The aim of the intellectual-business alliance urged by Simon, Kristol, and Powell was not just about reviving and recognizing their mutual interest in conservative, free enterprise ideology and ideas. It was about getting business to recognize its political power as an interest group—by urging it to exercise its economic power as a class. First and most immediate, Simon wrote, this would mean ending business support for all the liberal causes, and left-leaning faculty, that were aided and abetted through "mindless subsidizing of college and universities whose departments of economics, government, politics, and history are hostile to capitalism and whose faculties will not hire scholars whose views are otherwise."[24] But it also meant learning the lesson, as Lewis Powell put it in his memo to the Chamber of Commerce, "long ago learned by labor and other self-interest groups. This is the lesson that political power is necessary; that such power must be assiduously [sic] cultivated; and that when necessary, it must be used aggressively and with determination—without the reluctance which has been so characteristic of American business."[25] Ultimately, Simon acknowledged, the battle of ideas would have to be won in party politics as well as in the academy and boardrooms—beginning with a transformation in the Republican party from the vaguely business-oriented "Stupid Party" of compromising special interests to the party of principled free enterprise.[26] Perhaps most important for both Powell and Simon was for business to recognize that free enterprise, and liberty itself, was under siege from the reigning economic and regulatory orthodoxy—a recognition from which Simon himself, as a Wall Street executive and champion of the leveraged buyout, stood to gain. Indeed, in mounting the counteroffensive, the new foundations Simon envisioned would not be above the political fray. Irving Kristol put it bluntly in his own *Wall Street Journal* missive to corporate philanthropists: "when you give away your stockholders' money" he wrote, "your philanthropy must serve the longer-term interests of the corporation. Corporate philanthropy should not be, cannot be, disinterested."[27]

/ Kristol's column points to one final source of inspiration for the conservative foundations, this one as a catalyst as well as an unlikely model for countermobilization. The occasion for Kristol's column was a front-page headline announcement that shook the foundation world even as it provided fuel for the conservative fire—not in the least because it came from the belly of the beast, as it were. On January 11, 1977, Henry Ford II announced his resignation from the board of the Ford Foundation after thirty-three years of service, leaving it with no formal tie to either the Ford family or the Ford Motor Company, whose stock had been fully relinquished by 1974. In an earlier letter to board chairman and Vanderbilt University Chancellor Alexander Heard, key excerpts of which were released and widely reprinted in the press, Ford cited nothing more specific than his growing "sense of disengagement" as the reason for his departure, though his "parting thoughts" quickly became the subject of much speculation. Among other things, Ford pointed to the foundation's failure to scale back its programs in light of its recession-depleted endowment and to its retreat from experimentation in areas such as the arts. But the most provocative was his comment on the foundation's disengagement from the system of "competitive enterprise" that made it all possible. "In effect," he wrote, "the Foundation is a creature of capitalism," and yet it had become "hard to discern recognition of this fact in anything the foundation does. It is even more difficult to find an understanding of this in many of the institutions, particularly the universities, that are the beneficiaries of the Foundation's grant programs."[28] In the portion that became the *New York Times* quote of the day, Ford went on to insist that he was not "playing the role of the hard-headed tycoon who thinks all philanthropoids are socialists and all university professors are communists."[29] To the *Wall Street Journal* editorialists, however, Ford's departure spoke more

131

loudly than this caveat. It was a sign, they noted, not only of "the estrangement between business and that intellectual-academic-artistic community the Ford Foundation has done so much to subsidize and foster," but of the pervasive power and influence of the anticapitalist new class.[30]

Henry Ford's announcement did not spark a slew of sympathy resignations from foundation boards. Nor, despite staff speculation about the foundation's growing support for environmentalist and public interest law, could it be firmly established that some anticapitalist menace was to blame. After all, as the free enterprising journal *The Economist* noted, "[Ford President McGeorge] Bundy and his associates can hardly be described as hostile to business."[31] The resignation, however, did make a deep impression on conservative businessman John M. Olin and others who would become leading figures in the emerging conservative foundation movement. In fact, Olin's newly expanded and invigorated foundation would soon emerge as a leading force in the aggressive counterestablishment philanthropy envisioned in *A Time for Truth*.[32] For Simon, who in previously recorded transcribed interviews with ghostwriter Edith Efron had referred to the Ford Foundation staff as "liberal freaks," the timing was also fortuitous. About to depart Treasury to return to Wall Street, he had agreed to join the John M. Olin Foundation as board president.

Liberal foundations and Ford in particular would also prove catalytic for their philanthropic rivals, however inadvertently, in another way as well. More openly declaring an intention to "defund the left," the newly energized conservative foundations also set out to imitate what they saw as the left-liberal establishment's singular achievement. For all their contempt for those ultimate emblems of the liberal establishment, conservatives grudgingly admired what looked to them like the seamless networks of research, advocacy, and public interest law organizations they funded, and their consequent capacity to dominate the political agenda. It is significant that the lessons conservative foundations ascribed to and learned from their liberal counterparts were those that the liberal foundations would themselves eschew. One was to target elite institutions, in what amounted to a trickle-down approach to political change. The other was to have an agenda that went beyond the boundaries of what conventional politics would tolerate to bring about more fundamental change in political orientation.

Still, it was far more in countering than in emulating liberal philanthropy that the conservative foundations would make their mark. Nowhere did the dimensions of the counterstrategy play out more fully than in the John M. Olin Foundation. Along with the Lynde and Harry Bradley Foundation, it emerged as the most prominent of the "knowledgeable foundations" on the right. Originally established in 1953, the Olin Foundation was chiefly devoted to a combination of mainline charitable causes, antilabor groups, and small conservative colleges for much of its first two decades. Olin personally donated a good deal to his alma mater Cornell, where he sat on the board of trustees. By the early 1970s, though, retired and reportedly disgusted by what he saw as the Cornell administration's capitulation to "militant black radicals" in the student unrest of 1969, he began to think seriously about shifting the foundation's focus to a more aggressive defense of the free enterprise system he saw being challenged on campus.[33] Turning for staff work to his one-time chief labor negotiator Frank O'Connell, in 1973 Olin started laying the groundwork for what would become the core emphases of the foundation for the next thirty years. Under the headings public policy research, strategic and international studies, American institutions, and law and the legal system, the foundation's overriding purpose would be to strengthen the cultural as well as the economic and political underpinnings of the "American system of democratic capitalism." O'Connell, meantime, had consulted widely with leading conservative philanthropoids at the older Volker, Earhart, Koch Family, and Smith Richardson foundations, immersing himself in readings in free market political economy. It was O'Connell who later arranged for Hayek to contribute the foreword for Simon's book. O'Connell produced a lengthy memo laying out a course of action based chiefly on "supporting scholars and think tanks that favor limited government, individual responsibility, and a free society."[34] By 1977, the foundation was giving away nearly $1 million annually—modest in comparison to the Ford Foundation's $2.35 billion endowment and $160 million in expenditures, but a substantial increment in conservative philanthropic circles. It was also drawing attention for its grants to the likes of the Hoover Institution, the American Enterprise Institute, and Milton Friedman's hugely successful public television series based on his book *Free to Choose*. Launched as a free market answer to a popular series that John Kenneth Galbraith had hosted two years earlier, the series grew out of pressure to inject conservative thought into the otherwise "liberal" media. Interviewed in the *New York Times* at the time, Olin stated his ambition "to see free enterprise re-established in this country. Business and the public must be awakened to the creeping stranglehold that socialism has gained here since World War II." [35]

It was Simon, however, who would bring the foundation more fully into the conservative movement—largely by making it a vehicle for building the counterintelligentsia. As board president, Simon brought more structure, including a grant screening process, to what remained a small organization and, in the wake of Frank O'Connell's retirement in 1979, hired an executive director with neoconservative credentials. This was the Irving Kristol protégé Michael Joyce, then directing a joint Simon-Kristol venture, the Institute for Educational Affairs (IEA). [36]

Created in 1978 with start-up funds from such leading conservative philanthropies as the Olin, Scaife, JM, and Smith Richardson foundations, the IEA offers an early example of what, especially in its approach to knowledge, would distinguish this newly energized brand of conservative philanthropy from its mainstream counterpart. First, of course, was its explicitly ideological commitment. The IEA was set up to launch the conservative counterintelligentsia by steering corporate philanthropic dollars to conservative intellectuals. The idea was to combine Kristol's talent for spotting promising scholars with Simon's connections in the world of business and finance. Second was conservative philanthropy's equally self-conscious cultivation of a revolutionary or counterrevolutionary sensibility, a sensibility reflected not only in the proverbial war of ideas but also in the way conservative foundations carried it out. Thus, after failing to draw substantial corporate support (corporate foundations, for the most part, were too much invested in burnishing the company image for diverse constituencies), the IEA shifted its focus to funding the network of conservative student newspapers that had begun to crop up on elite campuses. That network would soon become a stepping stone for budding gadflies such as Dinesh D'Souza, who, with Olin funding and a perch at the American Enterprise Institute, would later go on to write truly incendiary attacks on the academy in *Illiberal Education* (1991). That was followed by a profoundly distorted and pseudo-historical attack on racial egalitarianism, *The End of Racism* (1996), that resurrected an old racist theme about the "civilizational" inferiority of blacks. More significant than such particulars was the broader shift that IEA's redirection indicates, toward creating institutional beachheads "on influential elite campuses—where, conservatives" believed, their ideas were most embattled. The legacy of this approach can be seen in a host of generously endowed university centers that bear the foundation's name and would nurture a great deal of the scholarship underlying the right-wing redirection of policy. Under the direction of Allan Bloom, philosophy professor and best-selling author of *The Closing of the American Mind* (1987), the University of Chicago's John M. Olin Center for Inquiry into the Theory and Practice of Democracy helped to spark a revival of the deeply antiliberal political philosophy of Leo Strauss, and more generally of an emphasis on the importance of moral virtue as the basis of the polity. Foundation staff members thought of the John M. Olin Institute for Strategic Studies at Harvard as another beachhead, principally in foreign policy. It was launched by political scientist Samuel Huntington, whose theoretical and academic critiques of liberal foreign policy and cultural assimilationism have been influential in some quarters on the right. As conservative beachheads, these and numerous other Olin-funded centers were meant to be platforms for conservative scholars and the student newspaper network as well as goads to the prevailing campus culture.

The Olin-funded beachheads that would prove most far-reaching, however, are associated with what is known as the law and economics movement. Itself inspired by the postwar preservation—then revival—of free-market and rational choice thinking in economics, the law and economics movement aimed to bring economic methods and principles to legal analysis and jurisprudence as well. Economic analysis, in the works of such leading proponents as Richard Posner and Richard Epstein, both affiliated with the University of Chicago Law School, would be used to maximize the values of economic efficiency and individual choice in the law. With more than $50 million in funding since 1977, the Olin Foundation subsidized the movement's more widespread institutionalization, from its original outposts at the University of Miami, George Mason University, and the University of Chicago to Harvard, Yale, Stanford, the University of Michigan, and Georgetown. More significant than its immediate business applications—for which it has drawn corporate as well as foundation support—this movement has provided the basic legal doctrine for deregulatory shifts in antitrust, environment, and other areas of law and policy.[37]

Yet a third distinguishing feature of the conservative "knowledgeable foundations" also stems from the counterrevolutionary sensibility. That brings us to the even more deeply subversive—subversive, that is, of liberal values—element of the war of ideas. This can be seen in Olin's pivotal role in what came to be known as the academic culture wars of the late 1980s and 1990s. In fact, they revived an older attack on the pragmatic roots of social scientific inquiry. The semiofficial opening shot was Allan Bloom's *Closing of the American Mind* in 1987, an attack on modern higher education funded with $50,000 from Olin. The book hit the best-seller lists, in no small part due to well-placed advance excerpts and sensation-making reviews. Along with a host of similarly themed books published at about the same time, Bloom bemoaned the decline of respect for, knowledge of, and education in the canon of western civilization. He was especially dismayed at the disappearing tenets of classical and natural law philosophy that, according to conservative critics, defined American civilization. In its place was a curriculum that had been taken over by what Roger Kimball called "tenured radicals" and that was designed to teach tolerance rather than truth, openness rather than absolutes, diversity rather than a common identity—steeped, that is, in the values of that old shibboleth of cultural relativism. Buoyed by the initial stir, Olin and other conservative foundations helped to turn the attack into a full-scale

136

culture war, with funds for books but also as a kind of fulcrum for the "public" conversation the right was framing—in such venues as the National Endowment of the Humanities under William Bennett and Lynne Cheney. D'Souza's *Illiberal Education* would only further stoke the flames, by going after affirmative action as well as the "politically correct" professoriate.

But Bloom's and other caricatures of the left-wing professoriate can also be seen as part of the older, longer culture war launched by the postwar right. Their barbs were not only aimed at the curriculum and the academy's embrace of diversity. On a more fundamental level, they were focused on discrediting an entire liberal epistemology, one that Bloom traced to John Stuart Mill and John Dewey and their emphasis on "liberalism without natural rights."[38] It was this turn in liberalism, Bloom argued, that separated knowledge from classical virtue and truth and that paved the way to cultural relativism and moral nihilism.

In Bloom, then, we can see a link between the academic and the older postwar culture wars that had singled out modern social science as an emblem of corrosive un-American values. But we can also see a final and critical element of the cultural work the right-wing foundations were accomplishing for the movement. Because if Bloom's *Closing of the American Mind* gave new life to a set of familiar ideas and charges, it brought the same to the old conservative narrative of western civilizational decline at the hands of a morally corrupt liberalism. It was a decline that in Bloom's as in countless similar narratives of the time reached its apotheosis in the 1960s. It was a decline that conservative foundations had set themselves to reverse in acting as agents of the counterrevolution.

By the late 1980s the Olin Foundation could claim to have had some hand in funding just about every significant application of conservative and neoconservative ideas to a much changed policy environment. In addition to the major institutional investments in expanding law and economics, conservative policy think tanks, and the culture wars, Olin support could be traced in the acknowledgments of an extraordinary number of the books that were said, like Charles Murray's *Losing Ground* in ending welfare, to have undermined tried and true liberal assumptions as they set new terms of debate on issues ranging from affirmative action, public education, and crime policy, to tort reform.[39] In support for such intermediary vehicles as the Federalist Society, a host of legal and legislative training institutes, and publications such as Irving Kristol's cold war revivalist *The National Interest*, Olin was ensuring that the ideas it was funding would be widely circulated to the people who would put them into practice. Its own trickle-down strategy of targeting elite institutions and audiences had brought an air of legitimacy to such untried and widely rejected ideas as supply-side economics. There was a sense, as Michael Joyce put it as early as 1981, that Ronald Reagan's election was a "kind of fruition" for the "ideals we've been supporting." Key to this sense of triumph, according to neoconservative scholar and philanthropoid Leslie Lenkowsky, was the devotion that united all the new breed of foundations—to the "future well-being of the system that gave rise to the foundations in the first place, namely capitalism."[40]

It was thus less in the individual components than in the overall shift in political culture that the Olin and other conservative foundations would more recently reflect on their collective success. The occasion for such reflection was unlikely as a cause for celebration, but long anticipated nonetheless. The Olin Foundation, having come to the end of the one-generation lifespan mandated by its founder, officially closed its doors in 2004. To its longtime executive director, James Piereson, that Olin actually could close its doors and withdraw what had become hundreds of millions in annual grants, was a sign that the larger conservative philanthropic movement had accomplished what it originally set out to do. Having steadily invested in the training grounds for a conservative new class, conservatives no longer felt so outnumbered, certainly not in the corridors of governance they had come to disdain. So, too, had they organized a highly effective counterintelligentsia, now anchored by a proliferating array of think tanks, advocacy organizations, and business interest law firms and institutes, that trafficked far less in empirical research than in ideas and ideological reformulations of key policy debates. The conservative foundations had also laid the groundwork for an expanding philanthropic network—in organizations, publications, seminars, and a fast-growing annual meeting sponsored by the Philanthropy Roundtable, itself an outgrowth of the IEA. Among its recent publications is the pamphlet *Soaring High*, which offers "fresh ideas" to potential donors interested in promoting "free market environmentalism."[41] With this infrastructure, and with an ever-widening source of wealthy donors ready to be advised, Piereson felt confident that the movement could well sustain itself without Olin funds.[42]

There was one other sign of success, though, that left Piereson wondering whether the movement would have the ballast necessary to maintain its energy. It was not just that the movement had become the dominant policy establishment. It was what, in his eyes anyway, that sea change signaled. Conservatism had become the dominant public philosophy, thanks in no small part to the work of foundation-funded movement intellectuals. What had for so long been a movement motivated and joined by opposition to liberalism—by a shared narrative of civilizational decline—could now tell a story of triumph and redemption. Having won the battle of ideas what, Piereson wondered, would be the future for conservative philanthropy?

It is a question, as I have argued, that liberal foundations might well turn toward themselves. Overstated though it may be, the success of the conservative philanthropic movement represents the triumph of a larger movement that has aimed to undermine a broadly pragmatic liberal project, including its mode of inquiry and its conviction that there is a collective public interest outside interests of a privatized market place. Modern conservatism, however, has also challenged the values of economic justice and democracy implicit in RSF's ongoing project of investigating inequality. For some, as I discuss in my conclusion, this challenge calls for a strategy of emulation and "learning" from the right. To me, it suggests the need for a response that draws on the deeper resources of the progressive and liberal reform traditions, and that begins by acknowledging what lies behind the questions we ask. It is a matter of recapturing the social question of the future by first reconnecting to the progressive past.

❧ CHAPTER 6 ❧

CONCLUSION

The controlling factor in any science is the way it views and
states its problems.
  —Robert S. Lynd, *Knowledge for What?*

In the opening chapters of this book, I addressed the enduring relevance of Progressive-era social knowledge by emphasizing its
origins in a social question that resonates powerfully with the challenges before liberal democracies today. No challenge links the two
eras more directly than the problem that has resumed its dubious
honor as the dominant social question of our time. It is a problem
that has become the arena for a growing number of multiracial reform coalitions since the early 1990s. It is a problem the Russell
Sage Foundation has for the past decade put at the center of its research agenda with its program on the Future of Work: the inequities and insecurities of "life and labor" in an era of massive
economic restructuring, globalization, and declining labor representation.[1]

As we saw in the case of the Pittsburgh Survey and the tradition
of inquiry it grew out of, the great achievement of the early Russell
Sage Foundation was not simply to document the manifold problems of life and labor. It was also to frame them as part of a sustained and broadly public conversation about the relationship between the social and economic conditions of industrial capitalism

and the institutions—indeed the meaning—of modern political democracy. In the process, the foundation made empirical social science a vital resource, one meant to find answers to those necessarily broad and inclusive questions and to broaden the conversation about what purposeful social action could achieve. As subsequently taken up by Robert Lynd and Gunnar Myrdal, and in the historical inquiries of W.E.B. Du Bois, the social question became the basis of a similarly purposive and empirical but now more consciously theoretical social knowledge—one capable of grappling with the deep-rooted dilemmas of race and inequality that continue to haunt us today.

But the work of Progressive-era social scientists is relevant for another reason as well, one that has more to do with the challenge discussed in part II, chapters 3 through 5. That challenge has confronted liberal social scientific philanthropy most directly in the emergence of a self-consciously counterrevolutionary knowledge establishment sustained by conservative movement philanthropy. It stems, however, from the more extended political and ideological crisis that has gripped late twentieth- and early twenty-first-century liberalism and that harks back to the similarly extended moment of ideological change and uncertainty that shaped social science at the early Russell Sage Foundation. Then, as now, the parameters of public philosophy were contested and the terms of social citizenship were in flux. The outcome of those at times fiercely contested battles was not at all clear. Then, too, deep-rooted and powerfully mobilized ideologies were part of the problem, in no small part because they generated fierce resistance to intervention in the market and to the very idea of shared social responsibility, and provided justifications for inequality. Progressive intellectuals responded with knowledge that was independent, objective, and challenging. They were willing both to ask probing questions and to be explicit about the values and principles and the more directive reform purposes that motivated their research.

That willingness to pursue knowledge that was at once objective and purposive is why the Progressive-era intellectuals are especially relevant today. The social science they envisioned is relevant at a time when the norms of public philosophy and social citizenship are once again being rewritten—not only by the vast social and economic transformations of global capitalism, but as well by the political and ideological transformations and in the moralized terms of the resurgent right. Even if they did not always succeed in their most ambitious reform aims, they did make social science that mattered as a tool for engaging fundamentally normative and ethical questions, questions of public philosophy and of social responsibility for the common good. To address such questions systematically and scientifically was not to confine the conversation to matters of empirical fact and scientific theory, but instead to use empirical fact and scientific theory to confront the culture with its most glaring ethical contradictions and to uphold the values of racial and economic democracy.

In recognizing the enduring relevance of the early Russell Sage Foundation and Progressive-era social knowledge, I do not mean to overlook the very real differences between our historical moments or to suggest that we can easily extract lessons from one historical era to another. Nor do I mean to overlook the limitations of those earlier inquiries or to exaggerate their importance in shaping public consciousness. I aim instead to establish a conversation between past and present about how contemporary, historically liberal social scientific philanthropies can respond more consciously and effectively to the profoundly altered ideological environment they now work in, and to the profoundly ideological challenge that the rise of the right has posed.

As should be clear by now, I do not see this as a challenge that can be dealt with by simply outstrategizing the right, as if to reduce it to a matter of somehow countering the counterintelligentsia. To do so would be to fall into the trap of allowing the right, once again, to dictate the terms of debate. It also assumes a level of ideological cohesion and a certain singularity of ideological purpose that the liberal foundations have been unwilling to impose, and that would more likely result in far narrower parameters than currently exist. It would be to fall back into the old trap of not taking the right seriously, in this instance by trivializing the deeper challenge that its rise to political power represents. That challenge, as I have argued, is not in the power of the "right ideas" but in the far more unsettling fact of their dominance in the absence of knowledge, and, just as often, in spite of knowledge to the contrary. Like so many others before and after it, when subjected to empirical scrutiny, Charles Murray's simple story blaming Great Society permissiveness for poverty, out-of-wedlock birth, and the underclass quickly fell apart. Its power as "higher truth" endured, however, and was (indeed, still is) subsequently and constantly reinforced by its absorption into the official logic of welfare reform.[2] The triumph of Murray's idea in turn brings up two other uncomfortable aspects of the right's success. One goes beyond the inability of empirical evidence to dislodge "higher truth" to the larger puzzle of why the generally liberal knowledge establishment has been so reluctant to assess the conservative counterrevolution as a set of ideological propositions, a vision for a well-ordered society, preferring instead to challenge its various claims on empirical grounds or to criticize it for being ideological. The other is the comparative difficulty liberal foundations have had in using their by-now impressive store of knowledge to shape a broader and sustained public conversation about the growing economic divide, not to mention to set in motion a different logic of reform.

In urging liberal foundations to reconnect to the Progressive-era past, then, I am drawing from two broadly historical conclusions about the philanthropic project of creating knowledge in the public interest, conclusions that are especially relevant to the challenge that the conservative counterrevolution presents today.

One is about what, historically, has mattered in making social science matter, not simply as the basis of improved understanding but also—and equally important—as the basis of a sustained public conversation about the problems of social and economic inequality. The social inquiry represented here by the Pittsburgh Survey and subsequent RSF-sponsored research was systematic, methodologically innovative, and remarkably well documented, in this sense claiming authority and social legitimacy from the scientific standards it met. As such, it was also convincing as a case for the value of knowledge that is grounded in social experience and evidence rather than in preordained truth, uninformed opinion, or prejudice. But, like Myrdal's *An American Dilemma*, those inquiries mattered not because of systematic social science alone. They mattered because they were motivated by a set of values and a sense of public purpose that in turn guided the questions social scientists were asking and indeed opened up new and unexamined areas for research. They mattered because they had a clear and broadly encompassing vision of the various publics to be addressed, one geared toward persuading not only the so-called experts and the politically well positioned but also the diverse citizenry they hoped to engage, including, to at least some (however inadequate) degree, the people they were writing about. A clear sense of public purpose, then, whether articulated as a commitment to social betterment or to racial justice, was what gave systematic social inquiry a broader relevance beyond the pursuit of better knowledge for its own sake. It is also what generated the rich array of visual tools and public venues through which the Progressive-era generation made it a point to make social science a part of an inclusive public conversation about social reform. Most important of all, what made those systematic inquiries matter was their ability to connect to a broader social question that, in its multiple variations, made the study of social problems public and collective rather than private and individualized.

My second historical conclusion builds on the first. It is about the vitally important role foundations can play—and the early Russell Sage Foundation in particular did play—in providing the social, institutional, and discursive space for creating a more socially purposive social science in a number of ways.

First is by becoming more conscious and deliberate about framing their work as part of the social question—the fundamentally normative question, that is, that underlies the more focused research questions social scientists ask.[3] Research questions are largely generated from the hypotheses and need to know of social science. The social question, on the other hand, is generated from the need to know of (broadly speaking) social reform, from the disparities between social realities and ideals, from concerns about social and economic disadvantage, and from (as Robert S. Lynd might have put it) what a modern democratic culture needs to know so not to subordinate its highest aspirations to the demands of powerfully organized interests or the exigencies of rapidly changing economic circumstances. Research questions concentrate on establishing the causes and consequences of declining wages, for example. The social question asks instead about the social meaning and value of wage-earning within the polity—and as such may well generate new questions for research. For foundations to ask the social question is thus not to relinquish their commitment to social science and to systematic inquiry as a way to deepen knowledge about social problems. It is, however, to recognize that the issues they choose for systematic inquiry are motivated by normative commitments and concerns.

Second, foundations can foster a more purposive social science by recognizing that the basic terms of and control over the social question are continually subject to contest and debate, and that contesting the terms of the now-prevailing social question is an important dimension of their work. Here again the issue is more than a matter of the competing angles of vision that emerge from social research. It is a matter of challenging the ideological assumptions— the vision of what the "good society" looks like, the respective obligations of citizens and the polity within it, and the values it should uphold—underlying the more and more privatized, individualized, deeply moralized, but also deliberately antiliberal version of the social question that has become embedded in contemporary poor law on the one side and in the new Gospel of Wealth on the other. It is at this level, the dominance over the social question, that conservative ideology has done most to undermine, and is in a position now to preempt, the efforts of liberal foundations to frame a public conversation about inequality.

A third step is for liberal foundations to be more conscious of the broadly cultural role they play in maintaining—and now in reestablishing—the legitimacy, not only of social science as such or of its role in the polity, but also of the intertwined ideas of acting in the public interest and for collective public social purposes that have been so thoroughly denigrated in the antigovernment rhetoric of the recent past.

Foundations can also play a role by thinking more carefully, and far more broadly, about the publics they seek to engage with social

145

scientific research. At the most basic level, this is a matter of more varied, comprehensive, and creative methods of dissemination—for which there are few better models than the extraordinarily rich and varied range of pamphlets, articles, popular journals, surveys, exhibits, maps, photographs, and (to borrow a phrase) "books, books, and more books" that the early Russell Sage Foundation used to get the word out about its research. It also, however, means engaging more systematically and deliberately with the many other voices and elements in civil society that are asking the social question as well, starting the conversation earlier in the research process, and sustaining it over a longer period. In this sense, the larger project of reframing the social question, of using it to begin a public conversation about inequality, starts with the recognition that social science alone cannot shoulder the task.

NOTES

Introduction

1. Hammack and Wheeler (1994).
2. On the "new liberalism" and social knowledge, see Mary Furner (1993, 171–241).
3. An important recent contribution is Sonja Amadae's *Rationalizing Capitalist Democracy* (2003).
4. Hodgson (1996).
5. Lynd (1939); Rose (1994).
6. Simon (1978, 231).
7. James Piereson, "You Get What You Pay For," *Wall Street Journal*, July 21, 2004.
8. On the rise of "advocacy tanks," see Andrew Rich (2004), Rich and Kent Weaver (1998), and Donald Abelson and Evert Lindquist (2000).
9. On conservative think tanks and their "revolutionary approach to ideas," see James Smith (1991, 22–23, 167–72).
10. Margaret Somers and Fred Block offer an illuminating discussion of conservative social naturalism and its historical role in welfare debates (2005). On the Victorian virtues, see Gertrude Himmelfarb (1995) and Joel Schwartz (2000).
11. In *Losing Ground*, Murray wrote: "Data are not essential to certain arguments about social policy and indeed can get in the way. The terms of debate can be grounded wholly in preferences about how the world ought to be, not how it is" (1984, 53).
12. Murray quoted in Tanner (1994, 8).
13. Smith (1991, 167–89; Rich and Weaver (1998, 235–53); Stefancic and Delgado (1996); David Callahan, "State Think Tanks on the Move," *The Nation*, October 12, 1998, p. 15-19.
14. Blank (2001).

Chapter 1

1. Kellogg (1909, 518, 521–22).
2. See, for example, Maurine Greenwald and Margo Anderson (1996).

3. On progressive intellectuals and social science, see Leon Fink (1997), Kevin Mattson (1998), and Ellen Fitzpatrick (1990). The idea and language of the public sphere is drawn from the philosopher Jurgen Habermas, whose best-known work is *The Structural Transformation of the Public Sphere* (1989).
4. Silverberg (1998).
5. In the large and growing literature on social science and the new liberalism leading sources include Mary Furner (1993, 2005), Dorothy Ross (1991), and Ira Katznelson (1996).
6. Haskell (1998).
7. Suskind (2004); Mooney (2005).
8. On the links between social science and a "reconstruction in political philosophy," see Mary Furner (2005).
9. Du Bois (1898).
10. For his turn away from social scientific empiricism, see W.E.B. Du Bois (1940).
11. La Guardia is quoted in Calder (1999, 124); Crocker (1999, 318–19). The RSF charter is reprinted in Glenn, Brandt, and Andrews (1947, 1:11).
12. Glenn, Brandt, and Andrews (1947, 1:3).
13. Glenn, Brandt, and Andrews (1947, 1:52). The panels are reproduced in the two-volume set as markers between chapters.
14. Chambers (1971).
15. Fitch (1909, 553).
16. Harrison, quoted in Byington (1910, 20).
17. Byington (1910, 179).
18. Eastman (1910, 152).
19. Butler (1909b, 570).
20. Wang (2005).
21. Quoted in James Smith (1991, 43).
22. Glenn, Brandt, and Andrews (1947, 2:532).
23. Glenn, Brandt, and Andrews (1947, 2:531).
24. Glenn, Brandt, and Andrews (1947, 2:531-45); Calder (1999, 287–90).
25. For a discussion of this and related work as part of a larger shift in the understanding of political economy, see Meg Jacobs (2004, 1999)
26. On the transatlantic reform networks during this period, see Daniel Rodgers (1998).
27. On Mary van Kleeck, see Guy Alchon (1991).
28. Odencrantz (1919).
29. Van Kleeck (1913).

30. Alchon (1998: 304–5).
31. Glenn, Brandt, and Andrews (1947, 1:153).
32. Selekman and van Kleeck (1925); Glenn, Brandt, and Andrews (1947, 2:379).
33. For an extended discussion of these studies, see Mark Hendrickson (2004).
34. Thompson and van Kleeck (1934).
35. Van Kleeck (1934).
36. Smith (1991, xiii).
37. Van Kleeck quoted in Hammack and Wheeler (1994, 50).

Chapter 2

1. Lagemann (1989).
2. Hawley (1974). On this growing research sector and its ideological orientation, see Guy Alchon (1985) and James Smith (1991).
3. On "scientism," see Dorothy Ross (1991).
4. President's Research Committee on Social Trends (1934, xciii–xcv).
5. Mark Smith makes this argument in *Social Science in the Crucible* (1994).
6. Hendrickson (2004).
7. Among the best known and most widely influential works have been C. Wright Mills, *The Sociological Imagination* (1959), Alvin Gouldner, *The Coming Crisis of Western Sociology* (1970), and Peter Novick, *That Noble Dream* (1988).
8. For example, see Helene Silverberg (1998).
9. Geary (2006).
10. Basil Manly, research director of the Commission on Industrial Relations, quoted in Lankford (1964, 30).
11. On the CIR, see Leon Fink (1997, 80–113), Mary Furner (1990) and Judith Sealander (1997, 224–34).
12. Walsh, quoted in Fink (1997, 98).
13. Van Kleeck, quoted in Hammack and Wheeler (1994, 50).
14. Park and Burgess (1925, 142-55).
15. Ogburn, quoted in Jackson (1990, 95).
16. Lagemann (1989); Smith (1991).
17. On Mitchell and the NBER, see Guy Alchon (1985) Mark Smith (1994, 64–70), and Ellen Lagemann (1989, 57–65).
18. Ross (1991, 443–44).
19. Furner (1975); Haskell (1998).

20. On politics by other means, see Mark Hendrickson (2004). On the disillusioning effects of World War I, see Dorothy Ross (1991, 320–26); Leon Fink (1997, 26–34).
21. On Hoover and his sponsorship of economic research for policy purposes, see Michael Bernstein (2001, 40–64).
22. Lynd (1939, 4).
23. On Lynd's career, see Mark Smith (1994, 120–58).
24. Lynd (1922).
25. The story of the encounter has been widely told, with some slight variations (Lynd 1992a, 1992b; Fox 1983; Mark Smith, 1994, 128–40).
26. As Mark Smith (1994, 140–41) points out, there were also other factors at work. The *Survey* articles had turned out to be good publicity for Rockefeller, who came off as responsive and humane. Lynd was also friendly with economist and child development expert Lawrence Frank, who as a foundation program officer was largely responsible for getting the Laura Spelman Rockefeller Memorial involved in that field, and who promoted Lynd for the job.
27. Lynd and Lynd (1929).
28. For an excellent discussion of *Middletown* and its reception, see Sarah Igo (2007, 23–35).
29. Smith (1994, 141–46).
30. Lynd's chapter, "The People as Consumers," was published as chapter 17 of the volume, over opposition from editor William Ogburn, who thought it too interpretive, and only after an extended debate within the editorial committee (President's Research Committee on Social Trends 1934).
31. For more on the thinking of "purchasing power progressives," see Meg Jacobs (2004).
32. Lynd (1939, 250).
33. Lynd (1939, 114–15).
34. Lynd (1939, 250).
35. Igo (2005).
36. For extensive discussion of the project that produced *An American Dilemma*, and Myrdal's role in it, see Walter Jackson (1990).
37. Jackson (1990, 56); Myrdal (1973, 293–307).
38. Myrdal (1973, 148).
39. Lynd (1944, 5).
40. Lynd (1944, 6).
41. Myrdal (1944, xlviii).
42. Myrdal (1944, lxi).

43. Myrdal (1944, lxxi).
44. On the process of coming up with the framework, its timing, and especially the influence of Myrdal's wartime experience in this regard, see Walter Jackson (1990, 135–64).
45. Myrdal (1944, 1045).
46. Myrdal (1944, 1045–57).
47. O'Connor (2001, 94-98; 2002).
48. The review was written in 1944, but remained unpublished for twenty years, until the release of Ellison's collection of essays *Shadow and Act* (Ellison, 1964).
49. Lagemann (1989, 146). On Myrdal's influence in later civil rights organizing and politics, see Sugrue (2004, 149).

Part II

1. See, for example, Eileen Applebaum, Annette Bernhardt, and Richard Murnane (2003).
2. Clayton (1996, 19).

Chapter 3

1. Anderson (2004); Miller (2006).
2. Cockett (1995).
3. For an extended discussion in the case of the anti-affirmative action battle, see Nancy MacLean (2006, 227–37).
4. Among the more incendiary, book-length attacks on the 1960s and the Great Society are Myron Magnet, *The Dream and the Nightmare* (1993) and Heather MacDonald, *The Burden of Bad Ideas* (2001).
5. Greider (2003).
6. Bell (1960). Francis Fukuyama (1992) later played on the "end of ideology" theme for much different purposes and in the much different context of the end of the Cold War. Fukuyama (2006) has more recently distanced himself from such formulations, and from neoconservative thought, in light of the war in Iraq.
7. On Kerr, Galbraith, and a host of other postwar intellectuals who thought about and debated the future of capitalism, see Nelson Lichtenstein (2006). John Kenneth Galbraith expresses his hopes for the New Class in *The Affluent Society* (1998, 243–54).
8. Editors of *Fortune* (1951).

9. On the cold war's impact on intellectual life, see Noam Chomsky (1997).
10. On the postwar social sciences and their institutionalization in Washington, see Hamilton Cravens (2004). On the policy sciences during this period more broadly, see Kenneth Prewitt (2005).
11. Gaither (1949).
12. Lagemann (1989, 147–51).
13. Longtime RSF staff member F. Emerson Andrews was a key figure in this emphasis, and later on in establishing the Foundation Center. See, for example, his *Philanthropic Foundations* (1956) and his memoir (1973).
14. Hammack and Wheeler (1994, 132).
15. Gilman (2004).
16. Mills (1943).
17. Smith (1991, 113–21).
18. O'Connor (1998).
19. Igo (2006).
20. The story is best told in Michael Bernstein, *A Perilous Progress* (2001).
21. Critchlow (1993).
22. Editors of *Fortune* (1951, 88).
23. Bell (1955).
24. Richard Hofstadter, "The Paranoid Style in American Politics," *Harper's Magazine,* November, 1964.
25. Neilsen (1972).
26. Cox Committee (1953).
27. Reece Committee report, reproduced in Wormser (1958, 114–19).
28. Reece Committee, in Wormser (1958, 323).
29. Quoted in Wormser (1958, vii).
30. Wormser (1958, 173, 199).
31. Wormser (1958, 288).
32. Meyer (1969, 96).
33. For further discussion of the hearings and the foundations' response, see O'Connor (2006).
34. Mirowski and Van Horn (forthcoming).
35. Hayek (1944); on Hayek, see Jerry Muller (2002, 347–87).
36. On Simons, and on the positive case for free market economics more generally, see Mirowski and Van Horn (forthcoming).
37. On the Mont Pelerin Society, see Godfrey Hodgson (1996), Max Hartwell (1995). On Fisher, see Richard Cockett (2004) and Alice O'-

Connor (2007); on British and U.S. think tanks, see Diane Stone (1996); and Adonis and Hames (1994).

38. Schumpeter's best known work, where he made these arguments about capitalism's "creative destruction" and the ultimately self-destructive aspects of capitalism, is *Capitalism, Socialism, and Democracy* (1942); see also Jerry Muller (2002, 288–316) for an especially compelling discussion of Schumpeter's use of irony.

39. Friedman (1962); Friedman and Friedman (1980).

40. Muller (2002, 377).

41. Weaver (1948). On Weaver, see Godfrey Hodgson (1996, 23–24), George Nash (1976, 30–36), and Roger Kimball ("The Consequences of Richard Weaver," *The New Criterion* vol. 25, September 2006, p. 4. http://www.newcriterion.com/archives/25/09/richard-weaver).

42. On Weaver's enduring significance as a rallying point, see Ted Smith (1998). The distinction between values and virtues later became a major theme in the work of Allan Bloom, among many other traditionalist conservatives, and can be seen in titles such as William Bennett's *The Book of Virtues* and Joel Schwartz, *Fighting Poverty with Virtue*.

43. Meyer (1969, 94).

Chapter 4

1. Murray (1984).

2. For the most hyperbolic version of the Murray story, see Tom Wolfe (2004). For a different take, see Alice O'Connor (2001, 247–50).

3. Indeed, as Murray's admirers are fond of pointing out, the *New York Review of Books* review essay by the sociologist Christopher Jencks featured a David Levine caricature of Murray in top hat, white tie, and tails, grinning with gleeful malice and greedily rubbing his hands ("How Poor Are the Poor?" vol. 32, no. 8, May 9, 1985).

4. Rich (2004).

5. Bray (2005, 59).

6. Block and Somers (2005).

7. For a summary and statistical overview of the so-called welfare explosion, see James Patterson (2000, 171–84).

8. Reagan (1974).

9. Mittelstadt (2004).

10. On the mixed motives behind welfare reform, and especially Nixon's FAP, see Alice O'Connor (1998).

11. Milton Friedman, F. A. Hayek, and other free market conservatives endorsed a minimal income guarantee as a way of replacing welfare and eliminating the need for the social welfare bureaucracy.
12. Reagan (1971); Reagan (1974)
13. "House Passes Radical Welfare Plan," *Human Events*, April 25, 1970, p. 6.
14. On Reagan's anti-FAP campaign, see Lou Cannon and Steven Hayward (1999).
15. Reagan, quoted in Booth (1970).
16. Reagan (1971).
17. Berkowitz (1991, 133–35); Reagan (1974, iv).
18. For a summary, see Alice O'Connor (1998).
19. McGirr (2001, 100).
20. Reagan (1974, iii–xiv).
21. Moynihan to Nixon, July 8, 1969. Nixon Project, NARA (II), WHCF WE Box 60. Moynihan's original memo was returned to him with Nixon's handwritten notation, circling the phrase "working poor" and indicating that he thought it an "excellent theme!"
22. *The Republican Battle Line*, v. 4 # 10, October 1970, p. 7; Booth (1970).
23. Agnew to Nixon, August 4, 1969. Moynihan Papers, Library of Congress, Box 275, folder 7.
24. Anderson (1978, 153–54).

Chapter 5

1. Lasch (1995).
2. Krehely, House, and Kernan (2004).
3. Kristol (1983, 1995). See also Walter Goodman, "Irving Kristol: Patron Saint of the New Right," *New York Times Magazine*, December 6, 1981, p. 90
4. O'Connor (1999).
5. Douglas and Wildavsky (1978).
6. For a recent discussion of the shift in the distribution of tax benefits, see David Johnston (2003).
7. Blumenthal (1988).
8. Brick (2006).
9. On the term "new class" and its use in conservative polemic, see Barbara Ehrenreich (1990) and Michael Lind (1996, 146–51).
10. Irving Kristol, "Business and the New Class," *Wall Street Journal*, May 19, 1975.

11. Friedman in Simon (1978, xii–xiii).
12. On the Powell memo, see David Hollinger (2000) and Oliver Houck (1984, 1457–60).
13. Powell (1971).
14. Packard, quoted in Miller (2006, 36–37).
15. Valerie Richardson, "The New Packard," *Philanthropy* November/December 2000.
16. Simon (1978, 230).
17. Simon (1978, 228–31).
18. Hayek to Simon, June 25, 1977. William E. Simon Papers, Lafayette College, Box 43, Folder 28; Hayek quoted in Simon (1978, xvi).
19. U.S. Catholic Bishops (1986); Miller (2006, 117–20).
20. On neoconservatism, see Peter Steinfels (1979), Godfrey Hodgson (1996), and Irving Kristol (1995).
21. Steinfels (1979, 7–12).
22. Walter Goodman, "Irving Kristol: Patron Saint of the New Right," *New York Times Magazine*, December 6, 1981, p. 90.
23. The editorial page recognized as much in "Grants and Groans," *Wall Street Journal*, January 14, 1977, p. 10.
24. Simon (1978, 231).
25. Powell (1971, 15).
26. Simon (1978, 238).
27. Irving Kristol, "On Corporate Philanthropy," *Wall Street Journal*, March 21, 1977, p. 18.
28. Henry Ford II to Alexander Heard, December 11, 1976. Ford Foundation Archives.
29. *New York Times*, January 12, 1977, A1.
30. "Grants and Groans," *Wall Street Journal*, January 14, 1977, p. 10.
31. "Ford Foundation: Charity Begins at Home," *The Economist*, January 22, 1977, p. 29; "In Its Forties, Ford Foundation Faces Change," *New York Times*, May 11, 1977, pp. B1, B4.
32. Miller (2003, 11–12); James Piereson, author interview, February 2004.
33. Miller (2003, 16); Smith (1991, 181–82).
34. Hayek to Simon, June 25, 1977. William E. Simon Papers, Lafayette College, Box 43, Folder 28; O'Connell, quoted in Miller (2003, 10).
35. Olin quote reported in *New York Times* obituary, September 10, 1982, p. D16; "Simon: Preaching the Word for Olin," *New York Times*, July 16, 1978, p. F1.
36. Piereson interview; Miller (2003, 13–14).
37. Teles (2007)

38. Bloom (1987, 29).
39. Eric Alterman, "The 'Right' Books and Big Ideas," *The Nation,* November 22, 1999.
40. Joyce and Lenkowsky quoted in Bernard Weinraub, "Foundations Assist Conservative Cause," *New York Times,* January 20, 1981, p. A25.
41. Bray (2005).
42. Piereson (2004).

Chapter 6

1. The Future of Work Program was initiated in 1994 as a joint project co-sponsored by the Russell Sage and the Rockefeller foundations.
2. For further discussion, see Alice O'Connor (2001, 247–50).
3. For an example of recent research that uses the social question as the starting point for empirical research, see Soss and Schram (2005).

REFERENCES

Abelson, Donald E., and Evert A. Lindquist. 2000. "Think Tanks in North America." In *Think Tanks and Civil Societies: Catalysts for Ideas and Action*, edited by James McGann and R. Kent Weaver. New Brunswick, N.J.: Transaction Publishers.

Adonis, Andrew, and Tim Hames, eds. 1994. *A Conservative Revolution?: The Thatcher-Reagan Decade in Perspective*. Manchester: Manchester University Press.

Alchon, Guy. 1985. *The Invisible Hand of Planning: Capitalism, Social Science, and the State in the 1920s*. Princeton, N.J.: Princeton University Press.

———. 1991. "Mary van Kleeck and Social-Economic Planning," *Journal of Policy History* 3(1): 1-23.

———. 1998. "The Self-Applauding Sincerity of Overreaching Theory: Biography as Ethical Practice, and the Case of Mary van Kleeck." In *Gender and American Social Science*, edited by Helene Silverberg. Princeton, N.J.: Princeton University Press.

Amadae, Sonja M. 2003. *Rationalizing Capitalist Democracy*. Chicago: University of Chicago Press.

Anderson, Brian, ed. 2004. *Turning Intellect into Influence: The Manhattan Institute at 25*. New York: Reed Press.

Anderson, Martin. 1978. *Welfare: The Political Economy of Welfare Reform in the United States*. Stanford, Calif.: Hoover Institution Press.

Andrews, F. Emerson. 1956. *Philanthropic Foundations*. New York: Russell Sage Foundation

———. 1973. *Foundation Watcher*. Princeton, N.J.: Princeton University Press.

Applebaum, Eileen, Annette Bernhardt, and Richard Murnane, eds. 2003. *Low-Wage America: How Employers Are Reshaping Opportunity in the Workplace*. New York: Russell Sage Foundation.

Bell, Daniel, ed. 1955. *The New American Right*. New York: Criterion Press.

———. 1960. *The End of Ideology: On the Exhaustion of Political Ideas in the Fifties*. New York: The Free Press.

Berkowitz, Edward D. 1991. *America's Welfare State: From Roosevelt to Reagan*. Baltimore, Md.: The Johns Hopkins University Press.

157

References

Bernstein, Michael A. 2001. *A Perilous Progress: Economists and Public Purpose in Twentieth-Century America*. Princeton, N.J.: Princeton University Press.

Blank, Rebecca M., and Ron Haskins, eds. 2001. *The New World of Welfare*. Washington, D.C.: Brookings Institution Press.

Block, Fred, and Margaret R. Somers. 2005. "From Poverty to Perversity." *American Sociological Review* 70(2): 260–87.

Bloom, Allan. 1987. *The Closing of the American Mind*. New York: Simon & Schuster.

Blumenthal, Sidney. 1998. *The Rise of the Counter Establishment: From Conservative Ideology to Political Power*. New York: HarperCollins.

Booth, Arch N. 1970. "An Open Letter About the Welfare Bill." Executive Vice President of the U.S. Chamber of Commerce, May 8, 1970. Photocopy in Moynihan Papers, Library of Congress, Box 279, Folder 7. Washington: U.S. Library of Congress.

Bray, Thomas J. 2005. "Soaring High: Strategies for Environmental Giving." Washington, D.C.: Philanthropy Roundtable.

Brick, Howard. 2006. "The Postcapitalist Vision in Twentieth-Century American Social Thought." In *American Capitalism: Social Thought and Political Economy in the Twentieth Century*, edited by Nelson Lichtenstein. Philadelphia: University of Pennsylvania Press.

Butler, Elizabeth Beardsley, 1909a. *Women and the Trades*. New York: Russell Sage Foundation.

———. 1909b. "The Working Women of Pittsburgh," *Charities and the Commons* XXI (January 2): 570.

Byington, Margaret. 1910. *Homestead: The Households of a Mill Town*. New York: Russell Sage Foundation.

Calder, Lendol. 1999. *Financing the American Dream: A Cultural History of Consumer Credit*. Princeton, N.J.: Princeton University Press.

Cannon, Lou, and Steven Hayward. 1999. "Welfare Reform: Another Win for the Gipper," Ashland, Ohio: Ashbrook Center for Public Affairs at Ashland University. http://www.ashbrook.org/publicat/oped/hayward/99/gipper.html.

Chambers, Clarke. 1971. *Paul U. Kellogg and the Survey: Voices for Social Welfare and Social Justice*. Minneapolis: University of Minnesota Press.

Chomsky, Noam. 1997. *The Cold War and the University: Toward an Intellectual History of the Postwar Years*. New York: The New Press.

Clayton, Obie, Jr., ed. 1996. *An American Dilemma Revisited: Race Relations in a Changing World*. New York: Russell Sage Foundation.

Cockett, Richard. 1995. *Thinking the Unthinkable*. New York: HarperCollins.

Cox Committee Report. 1953. *Final Report of the Select Committee to Investi-*

gate Foundations and Other Organizations. Washington: U.S. House of Representatives, 82nd Congress, 2nd sess.

Cravens, Hamilton, ed. 2004. *The Social Sciences Go to Washington: The Politics of Knowledge in the Postmodern Age.* New Brunswick, N.J.: Rutgers University Press.

Critchlow, Donald T. 1993. "Think Tanks, Antistatism, and Democracy." In *The State and Social Investigation,* edited by Michael Lacey and Mary O. Furner. New York: Cambridge University Press.

Crocker, Ruth. 1999. "The History of Philanthropy as Life History." In *Philanthropic Foundations: New Scholarship, New Possibilities,* edited by Ellen Condliffe Lagemann. Bloomington: Indiana University Press.

Douglas, James, and Aaron Wildavsky. 1978. "The Knowledgeable Foundation." In *The Future of Foundations: Some Reconsiderations,* edited by Landrum Rymer Bolling. Reprint, with commentary. New Rochelle, N.Y.: Change Magazine Press.

D'Souza, Dinesh. 1991. *Illiberal Education: The Politics of Race and Sex on Campus.* New York: Free Press.

———. 1996. *The End of Racism.* New York: Free Press.

Du Bois, W.E.B. 1898. "The Study of the Negro Problem." *Annals of the American Academy of Political and Social Science* 11(January): 1–23.

———. 1940. *Dusk of Dawn: An Essay Toward An Autobiography of a Race Concept.* New York: Schocken Books.

Eastman, Crystal. 1910. *Work-Accidents and the Law.* New York: Russell Sage Foundation.

Editors of *Fortune.* 1951. *U.S.A.: The Permanent Revolution.* New York: Prentice Hall.

Ehrenreich, Barbara. 1990. *Fear of Falling: The Inner Life of the Middle Class.* New York: Perennial.

Ellison, Ralph. 1964. *Shadow and Act.* New York: Random House.

Fink, Leon. 1997. *Progressive Intellectuals and the Dilemmas of Democratic Commitment.* Cambridge, Mass.: Harvard University Press.

Fisher, Antony. 1947. *The Case for Freedom.*

Fitch, John Andrews. 1909. "Some Pittsburgh Steel Workers." *Charities and the Commons* XXI (January 2): 553.

———. 1910. *The Steelworkers.* New York: Russell Sage Foundation.

Fitzpatrick, Ellen. 1990. *Endless Crusade: Women Social Scientists and Progressive Reform.* New York: Oxford University Press.

Fortune. 1951. *U.S.A. The Permanent Revolution.* New York: Prentice Hall.

Fox, Richard Wightman. 1983. "Epitaph for Middletown: Robert S. Lynd and the Analysis of Consumer Culture." In *The Culture of Consump-*

References

tion: Critical Essays in American History, 1880-1980, edited by Richard Wightman Fox and T.J. Jackson Lears. Durham: Duke University Press.

Friedman, Milton. 1962. *Capitalism and Freedom.* Chicago: University of Chicago Press.

Friedman, Milton, and Rose D. Friedman. 1980. *Free To Choose: A Personal Statement.* New York: Harcourt Brace.

Fukuyama, Francis. 1992. *The End of History and the Last Man.* New York: Free Press.

———. 2006. *America at the Crossroads: Democracy, Power, and the Neoconservative Legacy.* New Haven: Yale University Press.

Furner, Mary O. 1975. *Advocacy and Objectivity: A Crisis in the Professionalization of American Social Science.* Lexington: University of Kentucky Press.

———. 1990. "Knowing Capitalism: Public Investigation and the Labor Question in the Long Progressive Era." In *The State and Economic Knowledge: The American and British Experience,* edited by Mary O. Furner and Barry Supple. Cambridge: Cambridge University Press.

———. 1993. "The Republican Tradition and the New Liberalism: Social Investigation, State Building, and Social Learning in the Gilded Age." In *The State and Social Investigation in Britain and the United States,* edited by Michael J. Lacey and Mary O. Furner. New York: Woodrow Wilson Center Press and the Press Syndicate of the University of Cambridge.

———. 2005. "Structure and Virtue in United States Political Economy." *Journal of the History of Economic Thought* 27(1): 13–39.

Gaither, H. Rowan. 1949. *Report of the Study for the Ford Foundation on Policy and Program.* Detroit, Mich.: Ford Foundation.

Galbraith, John Kenneth. 1998. *The Affluent Society,* 40th anniv. ed. Boston and New York: Houghton Mifflin.

Geary, Daniel. 2006. "C. Wright Mills and American Social Science." In *American Capitalism: Social Thought and Political Economy in the Twentieth Century,* edited by Nelson Lichtenstein. Philadelphia: University of Pennsylvania Press.

Gilder, George. 1980. *Wealth and Poverty.* New York: Basic Books.

Gilman, Nils. 2004. *Mandarins of the Future: Modernization Theory in Cold War America.* Baltimore, Md.: The Johns Hopkins University Press.

Glenn, John M., Lilian Brandt, and F. Emerson Andrews. 1947. *Russell Sage Foundation, 1907-1946,* 2 vols. New York: Russell Sage Foundation.

Gouldner, Alvin. 1970. *The Coming Crisis of Western Sociology.* New York: Basic Books.

Greenwald, Maurine W., and Margo Anderson, eds. 1996. *Pittsburgh Surveyed: Social Science and Social Reform in the Early Twentieth Century.* Pittsburgh, Pa.: University of Pittsburgh Press.

Greider, William. 2003. "Rolling Back the Twentieth Century." *The Nation,* May 26, 2003.

Habermas, Jurgen. 1989. *The Structural Transformation of the Public Sphere.* Cambridge, Mass.: MIT Press.

Hammack, David C., and Stanton Wheeler. 1994. *Social Science in the Making: Essays on the Russell Sage Foundation, 1907-1972.* New York: Russell Sage Foundation.

Hartwell, R. Max. 1995. *A History of the Mont Pelerin Society.* Indianapolis, Ind.: Liberty Fund.

Hartz, Louis. 1955. *The Liberal Tradition in America .* New York: Harcourt Brace.

Haskell, Thomas L. 1998. *Objectivity is Not Neutrality: Explanatory Themes in History.* Baltimore, Md.: The Johns Hopkins University Press.

Hawley, Ellis. 1974. "Herbert Hoover, the Commerce Secretariat, and the Vision of an 'Associative State,' 1921–1928." *Journal of American History* 61: 116–40.

Hayek, Friedrich A. von. 1944. *The Road to Serfdom.* Chicago: University of Chicago Press.

Hendrickson, G. Mark. 2004. "Labor Knowledge and the Building of Modern Industrial Relations, 1918–1929." Ph.D. diss., University of California, Santa Barbara.

Himmelfarb, Gertrude. 1995. *The De-Moralization of Society: From Victorian Virtues to Modern Values.* New York: Alfred A. Knopf.

Hodgson, Godfrey. 1996. *The World Turned Rightside Up.* New York: Houghton Mifflin.

Hollinger, David A. 2000. "Money and Academic Freedom a Half-Century after McCarthyism: Universities amid the Force Fields of Capital." In *Unfettered Expression: Freedom in American Intellectual Life,* edited by Peggie J. Hollingsworth. Ann Arbor: University of Michigan Press.

Houck, Oliver A. 1984. "With Charity for All." *Yale Law Journal* 93(8)(July): 1415–1563.

Igo, Sarah. 2005. "From Main Street to Mainstream: *Middletown,* Muncie, and 'Typical America.'" *Indiana Magazine of History* 101(September): 239–58.

———. 2006. "'A Gold Mine and a Tool for Democracy': George Gallup, Elmo Roper, and the Business of Scientific Polling, 1935–1955." *Journal of Social and Behavioral Sciences* 42(2): 109–34.

References

———. 2007. *The Averaged American.* Cambridge, Mass.: Harvard University Press.

Jackson, Walter A. 1990. *Gunnar Myrdal and America's Conscience: Social Engineering and Racial Liberalism, 1938–1987.* Chapel Hill: University of North Carolina Press.

Jacobs, Meg. 1999. "Constructing a New Political Economy: Philanthropy, Institution-Building, and Consumer Capitalism in the Early Twentieth Century." In *Philanthropic Foundations,* edited by Ellen Condliffe Lagemann. Bloomington: Indiana University Press.

———. 2004. *Pocketbook Politics: Economic Citizenship in Twentieth-Century America.* Princeton, N.J.: Princeton University Press.

Johnston, David Cay. 2003. *Perfectly Legal: The Covert Campaign to Rig Our Tax System to Benefit the Super Rich—And Cheat Everybody Else.* New York: Penguin Books.

Katznelson, Ira. 1996. "Knowledge about What?: Policy Intellectuals and the New Liberalism." In *States, Social Knowledge, and the Origins of Modern Social Policies,* edited by Dietrich Rueschemeyer and Theda Skocpol. Princeton, N.J.: Princeton University Press.

Kellogg, Paul U. 1909. "The Pittsburgh Survey." *Charities and the Commons* XXI (January 2): 521–22.

———. 1914. *The Pittsburgh District: Civic Frontage.* New York: Russell Sage Foundation.

———. 1914. *Wage Earning Pittsburgh.* New York: Russell Sage Foundation.

Kleeck, Mary van. 1913. *Artificial Flower Makers.* New York: Russell Sage Foundation.

———. 1934. *Miners and Management.* New York: Russell Sage Foundation.

Krehely, Jeff, Meaghan House, and Emily Kernan. 2004. *Axis of Ideology: Conservative Philanthropy and Public Policy.* Washington, D.C.: National Committee for Responsive Philanthropy.

Kristol, Irving. 1983. *Two Cheers for Capitalism.* New York: New American Library.

———. 1995. *Neoconservatism: The Autobiography of an Idea.* New York: Free Press.

Lagemann, Ellen Condliffe. 1989. *The Politics of Knowledge: The Carnegie Corporation, Philanthropy, and Public Policy.* Chicago: University of Chicago Press.

Lankford, John. 1964. *Congress and the Foundations in the Twentieth Century.* River Falls, Wisc.: Wisconsin State University Press.

Lasch, Christopher. 1995. *The Revolt of the Elites and the Betrayal of American Democracy.* New York: W. W. Norton.

Lichtenstein, Nelson, ed. 2006. *American Capitalism: Social Thought and Political Economy in the Twentieth Century.* Philadephia: University of Pennsylvania Press.

Lind, Michael. 1996. *Up From Conservatism: Why the Right is Wrong for America.* New York: Free Press.

Lynd, Robert S. 1922a. "Crude-Oil Religion." *Harper's Monthly Magazine* 145(September): 425-34.

———. 1922b. "Done in Oil." *The Survey* 49(November): 137–46.

———. 1939. *Knowledge for What?* Princeton, N.J.: Princeton University Press.

———. 1944. "Prison for American Genius: 'The Vast and Ugly Reality of Our Greatest Failure.'" *The Saturday Review,* April 22, 1944, p. 5.

Lynd, Robert S., and Helen Merrell Lynd. 1929. *Middletown: A Study of Modern American Culture.* New York: Harcourt Brace.

———. 1937. *Middletown in Transition: A Study in Cultural Conflicts.* New York: Harcourt Brace.

MacDonald, Heather. 2004. *The Burden of Bad Ideas: How Modern Intellectuals Misshape Our Society.* New York: Ivan Dee.

MacLean, Nancy. 2006. *Freedom is Not Enough: The Opening of the American Workplace.* New York and Cambridge, Mass.: Russell Sage Foundation and Harvard University Press

Magnet, Myron. 1993. *The Dream and the Nightmare: The Sixties' Legacy to the Underclass.* New York: William Morrow.

Mattson, Kevin. 1998. *Creating a Democratic Public: The Struggle for Urban Participatory Democracy During the Progressive Era.* University Park: Pennsylvania State University Press.

McGirr, Lisa. 2001. *Suburban Warriors.* Princeton, N.J.: Princeton University Press.

Meyer, Frank. 1969. *The Conservative Mainstream.* New Rochelle, N.Y.: Arlington House.

Miller, John J. 2006. *A Gift of Freedom: How the John M. Olin Foundation Changed America.* San Francisco, Calif.: Encounter Books.

———. 2003. *Strategic Investment in Ideas: How Two Foundations Reshaped America.* Washington, D.C.: Philanthropy Roundtable.

Mills, C. Wright. 1943. "The Professional Ideology of Social Pathologists." *American Journal of Sociology* 49(2): 165–80.

———. 1959. *The Sociological Imagination.* New York: Oxford University Press.

Mirowski, Philip, and Robert Van Horn. Forthcoming. "The Rise of the

References

Chicago School." In *The Making of the Neoliberal Thought Collective,* edited by Philip Mirowski and Dieter Plehwe. Cambridge: Harvard University Press.

Mittelstadt, Jennifer. 2004. *From Welfare to Workfare.* Chapel Hill: University of North Carolina Press.

Mooney, Chris. 2005. *The Republican War on Science.* New York: Basic Books.

Muller, Jerry Z. 2002. *The Mind and the Market.* New York: Alfred A. Knopf.

Murray, Charles. 1984. *Losing Ground: American Social Policy, 1950-1980.* New York: Basic Books.

Myrdal, Gunnar. 1944. *An American Dilemma: The Negro Problem and Modern Democracy.* New York: Harper and Row.

———. 1965. *The Political Element in the Development of Economic Theory.* New York: Routledge.

———. 1973. *Against the Stream.* New York: Pantheon Books.

Nash, George. 1976. *The Conservative Intellectual Movement in the United States.* New York: Basic Books.

Neilsen, Waldemar A. 1972. *The Big Foundations.* New York: Columbia University Press.

Novick, Peter. 1998. *That Noble Dream: The "Objectivity Question" and the American Historical Profession.* New York: Cambridge University Press.

Nugent, Rolf. 1939. *Consumer Credit and Economic Stability.* New York: Russell Sage Foundation.

O'Connor, Alice. 1998. "The False Dawn of Poor-Law Reform: Nixon, Carter, and the Quest for a Guaranteed Income." *Journal of Policy History* 10(1): 99–129.

———. 1999. "The Ford Foundation and Philanthropic Activism in the 1960s." In *Philanthropic Foundations: New Scholarship, New Possibilities,* edited by Ellen Condliffe Lagemann. Bloomington: Indiana University Press.

———. 2001. *Poverty Knowledge: Social Science, Social Policy, and the Poor in Twentieth Century U.S. History.* Princeton, N.J.: Princeton University Press.

———. 2002. "Foundations, Research, and the Construction of 'Race Neutrality.'" *Souls* 4(1): 54-62.

———. 2006. "The Politics of Rich and Rich: Postwar Investigations of Foundations and the Rise of the Philanthropic Right." In *American Capitalism: Social Thought and Political Economy in the Twentieth Century,* edited by Nelson Lichtenstein. Philadelphia: University of Pennsylvania Press.

————. 2007. "The Privatized City: The Manhattan Institute, The Urban Crisis, and the Conservative Counterrevolution in New York." *Journal of Urban History*. Forthcoming.

Odencrantz, Louise C. 1919. *Italian Women in Industry*. New York: Russell Sage Foundation.

Park, Robert E., and Ernest W. Burgess. 1925. *The City: Suggestions for Investigation of Human Behavior in the Urban Environment*. Chicago: University of Chicago Press.

Patterson, James. 2000. *America's Struggle Against Poverty in the Twentieth Century*. Cambridge, Mass.: Harvard University Press.

Piereson, James. 2004. "The Conservative Foundation Movement—Past and Future," Speech delivered to the annual meeting of the State Policy Network. Chicago, Illinois (April 29, 2004).

Powell, Lewis F., Jr. 1971. "Attack of Free Enterprise System." Confidential Memorandum from Lewis F. Powell to Eugene B. Sydnor, Jr., Chairman, Education Committee, U.S. Chamber of Commerce (August 23, 1971). Reprint. Minneapolis, Minn.: Media Transparency. http://www.media-transparency.org/story.php?storyID=22.

President's Research Committee on Social Trends. 1934. *Recent Social Trends: Report of the President's Research Committee on Social Trends*, one volume edition. New York: Whittlesey House.

Prewitt, Kenneth. 2005. "Political Ideas and a Political Science for Policy." *Annals of the American Academy of Political and Social Science* 600(July): 1–16.

Reagan, Ronald. 1971. *Meeting the Challenge: A Responsible Program for Welfare and Medi-Cal Reform*. Transmitted to the California Legislature March 3, 1971.

————. 1974. *California's Blueprint for National Welfare Reform: Proposals for the Nation's Food Stamp and Aid to Families with Dependent Children Programs* (September). Series XI, Box GO143. Simi Valley, Calif.: The Ronald Reagan Presidential Library and Museum.

Reece Committee Report. 1955. *Final Report of the Special Committee to Investigate Tax-Exempt Foundations and Comparable Organizations*. Washington: U.S. House of Representatives, 83rd Congress, 2nd sess.

Rich, Andrew. 2004. *Think Tanks, Public Policy, and the Politics of Expertise*. New York: Cambridge University Press.

Rich, Andrew, and R. Kent Weaver. 1998. "Advocates and Analysts: Think Tanks and the Politicization of Expertise in Washington." In *Interest Group Politics*, edited by Allan Cigler and Burdett Loomis. Washington: Congressional Quarterly Press.

References

Richmond, Mary. 1917. *Social Diagnosis*. New York: Russell Sage Foundation.

Rodgers, Daniel T. 1998. *Atlantic Crossings: Social Politics in a Progressive Age*. Cambridge, Mass.: Harvard University Press.

Ross, Dorothy. 1991. *The Origins of American Social Science*. New York: Cambridge University Press.

Schumpeter, Joseph A. 1942. *Capitalism, Socialism, and Democracy*. New York: Harper and Brothers.

Schwartz, Joel. 2000. *Fighting Poverty with Virtue: Moral Reform and America's Urban Poor, 1825–2000*. Bloomington: Indiana University Press.

Sealander, Judith. 1997. *Private Wealth and Public Life: Foundation Philanthropy and the Reshaping of American Social Policy from the Progressive Era to the New Deal*. Baltimore: Johns Hopkins University Press.

Selekman, Ben M., and Mary van Kleeck. 1925. *Employees' Representation in Coal Mines*. New York: Russell Sage Foundation.

Silverberg, Helene, ed. *Gender and American Social Science: The Formative Years*. Princeton, N.J.: Princeton University Press, 1998.

Simon, William E. 1978. *A Time for Truth*. New York: Reader's Digest Press.

Smith, James A. 1991. *The Idea Brokers: Think Tanks and the Rise of the New Policy Elite*. New York: Free Press.

Smith, Mark C. 1994. *Social Science in the Crucible: The American Debate Over Objectivity and Purpose, 1918–1941*. Durham, N.C.: Duke University Press.

Smith, Ted J., III, ed. 1998. *Steps toward Restoration: The Consequences of Richard Weaver's Ideas*. Wilmington, Del.: ISI Books.

Soss, Joe and Sanford Schram. 2005. "Coloring the Terms of Membership: Reinventing the Divided Citizenry in an Era of Neoliberal Paternalism." Paper prepared for the conference on The Color of Welfare. University of Michigan. September.

Stefancic, Jean, and Richard Delgado. 1996. *No Mercy*. Philadelphia, Pa.: Temple University Press.

Steinfels, Peter. 1979. *The Neoconservatives: The Men Who Are Changing American Politics*. New York: Simon & Schuster.

Stone, Diane. 1996. *Capturing the Political Imagination: Think Tanks and the Policy Process*. London: Frank Cass.

Sugrue, Thomas J. 2004. "Affirmative Action from Below: Civil Rights, the Building Trades, and the Politics of Racial Equality in the North, 1945-1969." *Journal of American History* 91(1): 145-73.

Suskind, Ron. "Faith, Certainty, and the Presidency of George W. Bush." *New York Times Magazine*. October 17, 2004.

Tanner, Michael. 1994. *Ending Welfare as We Know It.* Policy Analysis # 212 (July 7, 1994). Washington, D.C.: The Cato Institute. http://www.cato.org/pubs/pas/pa-212.html.

Teles, Steven M. 2007. *The Evolution of the Conservative Legal Movement.* Princeton: Princeton University Press.

Thompson, William O., Mary van Kleeck, and Earl Browder. 1934. *The NRA from Within: The Communist Position.* New York: International Pamphlets.

U.S. Catholic Bishops. 1986. *Economic Justice for All.* Washington, D.C.: USCC Office for Publishing and Promotion Services.

Wang, Jessica. 2005. "Imagining the Administrative State: Legal Pragmatism, Securities Regulation, and New Deal Liberalism." *Journal of Policy History* 17(3): 257–93.

Weaver, Richard. 1948. *Ideas Have Consequences.* Chicago: University of Chicago Press.

Wolfe, Tom. 2004. "Revolutionaries," reprinted as "The Manhattan Institute at Twenty-Five." In *Turning Intellect into Influence: The Manhattan Institute at 25,* edited by Brian Anderson. New York: Reed Press.

Wormser, Rene A. 1958. *Foundations: Their Power and Influence.* New York: Devin-Adair.

INDEX

Boldface numbers refer to figures and tables.

Index